THE NEXT BIG INVESTMENT BOOM

Learn the secrets of investing
from a master and
how to profit from
COMMODITIES

MARK SHIPMAN

London and Philadelphia

Commodity investments can go down as well as up. This book was completed in 2005, but market conditions change and past performance is not a guarantee of future results. Neither the publisher nor the author accepts any legal responsibility for the contents of the book, which is not a substitute for detailed professional advice. Readers should conduct their own due diligence into the commodity markets and their investment activity through an appropriately authorized company.

Publisher's note

Every possible effort has been made to ensure that the information contained in this book is accurate at the time of going to press, and the publishers and authors cannot accept responsibility for any errors or omissions, however caused. No responsibility for loss or damage occasioned to any person acting, or refraining from action, as a result of the material in this publication can be accepted by the editor, the publisher or the author.

First published in Great Britain and the United States in 2006 by Kogan Page Limited
Reprinted in 2006

120 Pentonville Road
London N1 9JN
United Kingdom
www.kogan-page.co.uk

525 South 4th Street, #241
Philadelphia PA 19147
USA

© Mark Shipman, 2006

The right of Mark Shipman to be identified as the author of this work has been asserted by him in accordance with the Copyright, Designs and Patents Act 1988.

ISBN 0 7494 4577 7

British Library Cataloguing-in-Publication Data

A CIP record for this book is available from the British Library.

Library of Congress Cataloging-in-Publication Data

Shipman, Mark.
    The next big investment boom : learning the secrets of investing from a master and how to profit from commodities / Mark Shipman.
        p. cm.
    Includes index.
    ISBN 0-7494-4577-7
    1. Investments. 2. Commodity exchanges. I. Title.
HG4521.S525 2006
332.64'4—dc22
                                    2005037498

Typeset by JS Typesetting Ltd, Porthcawl, Mid Glamorgan
Printed and bound in Great Britain by Cambrian Printers Ltd, Aberstwyth, Wales

Contents

About the author

Mark Shipman is a highly successful investor and has made a personal fortune from backing his own judgement with his own money. He has been in the financial industry since 1979. Initially joining a major international investment bank and training in accountancy, he was rapidly promoted to the dealing room where he specialized in futures and options. In 1990, he left the City to establish one of the UK's first hedge fund management companies and the following year achieved personal success by winning the World Professional Futures Trading Championship.

In addition to participating in long-term investment trends, Mark also consults to numerous City institutions including banks, brokers, hedge funds, headhunters, venture capitalists and even the UK financial regulator. His weekly investment diary can be found on the www.trend-follower.com website.

Away from the world of finance, Mark is an accomplished tournament poker player and a highly successful racehorse owner/breeder, with his distinctive maroon and light blue racing colours recently carried to victory in one of Europe's richest races.

Foreword

Jack Welch, the former CEO of General Electric, once said that the two most important ingredients for success are 'focus and drive'. Perhaps without realizing it, Mark Shipman possesses both in abundance. In 25 years in the City I have rarely met a trader or investor who has consistently been able to identify future market trends as well as Mark has been able to do.

As with most really successful people, Mark has put in a tremendous amount of hard work to perfect the strategies that he uses today, and anybody reading this book will gain an enormous advantage in their own approach to investing. He combines fundamental awareness with sound technical analysis and this has resulted in a diverse crop of macro-trend successes, including stock market indices, individual shares, bonds and property. Investment success in such a wide variety of assets is sound testimony to the robustness of his analysis, and although these are relatively early days in the commodity market revival, it would appear that he has identified yet another hugely profitable macro trend.

The notes in the 'About the Author' section of the book contain one glaring omission about Mark: he is a highly accomplished, self-taught drummer, having once played with a well-known 80s pop group. Everybody will know the key ingredient for a drummer is a keen sense of timing, and it can be no coincidence that he has developed an investment style that places great emphasis upon the 'timing' aspect of participating in long-term trends. It is perhaps ironic that Mark's investment strategies allow him to 'avoid the noise'. He has never knowingly avoided the noise when drumming!

As a professional investor, I can identify very closely with the need to avoid the 'emotional burn-out' to which Mark refers and I would urge all who have purchased this book to read and re-read 'Appendix B – An Interview with Mark Shipman'. The sentiments expressed in this piece will prove to be both enlightening and key to any future success that the reader will enjoy, be it in commodities or any other asset class.

Today's world provides an unprecedented amount of facts, statistics and general market commentary, which has created a syndrome known as 'information overload' amongst the investment community. What Mark has realized is that it's impossible to keep track of all this fundamental information, indeed to do so would create exhaustion and possibly confusion. Instead, he has created an approach that is more a study of human nature and behaviour, which remains constant in a fast and often transient world. By keeping the analysis simple he has opened the door to successful investing for anybody who can find an hour or two a week to look after their finances.

At a fundamental level, I believe that we are in the early stages of a shift from pieces of paper called currencies into a world where traditional commodities are, once again, a more important and lasting store of value.

With that in mind, absorb and enjoy this book.

Jonathan Chapman
Professional Investor and Former Head of Trading,
Standard Chartered Bank

Acknowledgements

Before we go any further, there are a number of special people to whom I owe a major debt of gratitude for their help, advice and timely support throughout my career in finance, fund management and investing. I am eternally grateful to (in alphabetical order): Rupert Allan, Phil Bellanti, Frank Burgess, Allen Cheng, Steve Ciampi, Brian Cornell, Carol Dickman, Sandra D'Italia, Sean Doyle, David Elkin, Frank Franiak, Dick Grace, James Green, Karl and Barbara Gysin, Mike Harkins, Matt Johnson, Richard Kovner, Ashley Levett, Melvin Mardell, Nicola Meadon, Bill O'Heron, Jeremy Parfit, Lois Peltz, Scott Ramsey, Mike Schaefer, Gerry Sharma, Grace and Bill Sullivan, Ray Thompson, Fritz and Elle Uthe, Rose and Bill Young.

In addition, I would also like to thank the following for their help, support and encouragement with the publication of this book (again, in alphabetical order): Bill Bonds, David Buik, Toby Carr, Jon Chapman, Dave Corner, Manus Cranny, Pauline Goodwin, Chris Hill, Ian Jenkins, Chris Johnson, Pat Lomax, George Marshall, Mel Mayne, Stuart Newton, The Petersens, Lol Pryor, Dr Herman Wang, Juliet Wedderburn and especially my dad, Frank, who must have read and reread all of the ninety odd drafts and my wife, Sandra, for resurrecting her typing skills when I needed them most.

And finally, I'd like to thank Equis International Inc of Salt Lake City, Utah (www.equis.com) for the use of their excellent Metastock software charts in this book.

I would like to thank my mum, my dad, my wife and my daughter for all their love and support throughout the years and I dedicate this book to them.

Introduction

In recent history there have been two major investment booms, namely in technology stocks and property. Both were extremely rewarding for those who were able to spot the trends early enough and didn't outstay their welcome at the end. However, investors are now struggling to find anything that will provide them with a decent return. The most recent boom in residential property appears to have 'shot its bolt' with values now beginning to readjust to more realistic levels, and although conditions have improved for the stock market it still languishes well below its previous highs with little prospect of a sustainable major bull market developing soon. You can't even get a decent return from deposit accounts or bonds with interest rates so low. So, where can one look?

Commodities. Yep, *stuff* like gold and oil and sugar and cotton. Not very sophisticated, not very modern, not very exciting, you might think, but you'd be wrong.

Despite the phenomenal and well-documented recent rise in the price of oil and its related products, you may be surprised to learn that on an inflation-adjusted basis commodity prices are at their lowest levels since the Great Depression of the 1930s.

Picking the bottom of any market is always a dangerous game. Therefore, before I invest, I like to see evidence that prices have turned upwards before participating. A quick review of the inflation-adjusted chart of the commodity-based CRB Index as shown in Figure 0.1 confirms that this upward momentum has now begun and I believe this could be just the beginning of one of the biggest investment bull

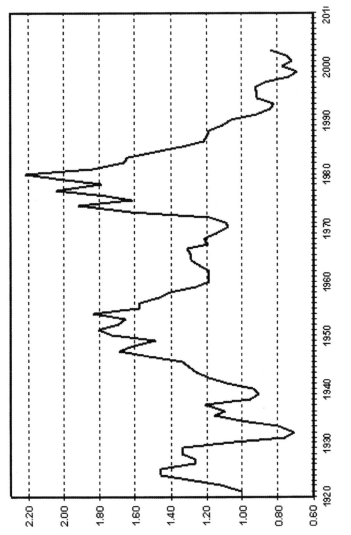

Commodities near all-time low

Source: Di Tomasso Group

Figure 0.1 Inflation-adjusted commodity prices 1920–2005

markets in history. Even if you have never invested in commodities or never intend to, the implication of such a massive rise in their value will affect every one of us and, for the unprepared, the future could not only be a lost opportunity to make money but it could also see an erosion of your wealth. High commodity prices will mean the return of high inflation and ultimately the return of high interest rates.

However, it's not all doom and gloom. If you decide to participate in the forthcoming commodity boom, you can protect yourself from the effects of high inflation and make some serious money as well, and I make the following prediction:

> Tomorrow's new millionaires and billionaires will create their fortunes not from computer technology, software, the internet, mobile phones or property but from commodities and commodity-related businesses.

In this book, I'm going to show you which markets to look at, what's creating the shift in their values and how to participate in them. The reason most investors make bad decisions is through lack of knowledge, so the more educated you can become about investing your money, the better your chances of not only avoiding bad investment products and advice but also of participating in the right investments at the right time and making yourself some decent money.

Aside from your own personal health and that of your loved ones, nothing is more important than ensuring you are financially equipped to have a comfortable life. Money may not buy happiness but it's great at removing most of life's stresses, and, let's face it, it doesn't matter whether you are in your 20s, 30s, 40s, 50s, 60s or 70s, it's never too early or too late to try to make a bit more money.

But first...

Take responsibility for your money

Your future!?

I always assumed that if I worked hard and paid my contributions I would get a decent pension. Now I've been proved horribly wrong.

Financial Mail on Sunday, 17 March 2002

You saved for it. You earned it. You worked your whole life for it. Why has the money DISAPPEARED?

Saga Money, Spring 2003

Alarm as pensions black hole hits £91 billion

Metro, 31 March 2003

Actuary faces first pensions advice lawsuit

The Times, 17 April 2003

Why millions might have to work to 70s

Daily Mail, 1 March 2003

The majority of the working population will spend over 75,000 hours at work and, even on average earnings, will earn over £1 million in wages. However, when it comes to retiring there is a high probability that very little of this money will be left. I'm afraid it's a sad fact that most people never achieve their true potential for building wealth and anyone who reads the financial press or flicks through the financial section of their daily paper will be only too aware that the future holds a major problem for millions of hard-working people. It is also one of the reasons I decided to write this book. It is not my intention to cause alarm or unnecessary worry for those near retirement but there could be a nasty surprise for those who are unprepared.

In a recent article, the *Financial Mail on Sunday* revealed the shocking statistic that 58,000 company pension schemes have been wound up over the past 10 years because they were unable to pay the pensions they promised. The Occupational Pensions Regulatory Authority, which compiled these statistics, goes on to warn that a further 30,000 schemes are under threat. In addition, a survey published by investment bank Morgan Stanley estimates that Britain's largest companies are facing an £85 billion shortfall in their pension schemes. Yes, £85 billion. This means thousands upon thousands of decent, hard-working people are at risk and that's why I want to draw your attention to the subject of your future and, in particular, how you plan to finance your retirement. Many expect a state, company or other pension scheme to provide the necessary cash, and for a few this may well be enough, but for a large percentage the previously mentioned newspaper headlines may unfortunately ring true.

When you consider that the majority of wealth is created from investment income rather than employment income, it makes sense to focus more of your time on where you are going to invest your money than on how you can earn more of it. If people would only devote more time to educating themselves about investing, things could be so very different. You owe it to yourself to take control of your financial planning and your financial future. It is the only way you can successfully avoid becoming one of the unfortunate newspaper statistics.

Let's assume you have taken on-board my recommendation. What now? You are now an investor and this book has been written especially for you.

Self-directed investing

Blame Nobody. Expect Nothing. Do Something.

New York Giants locker-room motto

Taking control

It's my opinion that, by adopting the right mental attitude and strictly following strategies that force you to invest in assets that are appreciating in value and liquidate assets that are falling, it is possible for a complete novice to achieve outstanding returns: 'investing, where the smart money isn't so smart, and the dumb money isn't really as dumb as it thinks' (Peter Lynch, fund manager and author of *One Up on Wall Street*).

Instead of burying your head in the sand when the subject of finance or investing comes up, you need to make the effort to understand the subject. It really isn't as complicated as some people would have you believe and you could gain a lifetime's financial security for just a few hours' study. You need to look after your money because it will not look after itself.

Investing isn't trading

Please note this book is intended to help you become an investor, not to help you trade, and there are major differences between the two.

Trading is a completely different game that has its own set of demands and is generally conducted by hard-nosed individuals, known as 'speculators', who take numerous short-term positions for smaller profits rather than attempting to catch major longer-term price trends from just one or two positions. I personally define 'long-term' as any market movement that takes months or years to unfold and 'short-term' as any period less than this down to price fluctuations that occur over just a few minutes. Trading is a career, a profession, a full-time job, whereas investing should be conducted in addition to how you earn your regular income. Trading is about income whereas investing is about long-term capital gain. I'm an investor and not a trader because experience has taught me it is far easier to profit from where the price of an asset is heading over the next few months and years than over the next few days, hours or even minutes. This is because long-term price movements are influenced by long-term economic fundamentals, which tend not to change that quickly, thereby creating more consistent price trends. In contrast, shorter-term price movements are often the result of emotional buying and selling panics due to news events and this makes them far more random in nature and extremely unpredictable. Unless you have had years of experience and also have the time needed to make trading your career, I recommend you focus on long-term market trends and make sure that you are an investor. Long-term investing is comparatively less time consuming, less stressful and usually more financially rewarding.

What's required

Just by purchasing this book, you have made an important step towards changing your financial future but you still have to read it and apply the information it contains. Statistically, only a small percentage of readers ever complete the reading of any book they purchase, be it *War and Peace* or a child's book of painting by numbers. So, just by making the effort to read this little book and digest its contents you're already distancing yourself from the vast majority who are always complaining that opportunities seem to pass them by. In other words, you have to be prepared to help yourself before anyone else can. This book is designed to educate and inform, not collect dust in your house, fill the space of an empty drawer or act as a doorstop. Use it correctly and, you never know, it might just change your life for the better.

To be a successful investor, whether you invest in property, the stock market or other assets, you will need to have a basic understanding of the following:

- the psychological pressures you will encounter by placing your own money at risk and assuming the responsibility for both good and bad performance;
- investment strategies that force you to participate in the direction of the long-term trend;
- how an investment boom or bubble evolves and how to identify when it's ending.

Just as important is what you don't need. You don't need a degree in economics; you don't need to attend one of those £2,000-a-day seminars held by unheard-of 'experts'; you don't need to take out expensive subscriptions for up-to-the-minute market data; and you definitely don't need a pin-stripe suit!

Successful investing doesn't require above-average intelligence because it is not an intellectual challenge; it is an emotional one and, I believe, it is a challenge most of you are capable of meeting head on and winning. If there's anything 'clever' about what I do, it is recognizing what works and ignoring what doesn't. I left school at 16 without a GCE O level in mathematics, never studied economics and still haven't. So, if I can do this, anyone can. In summary, all you really need to possess is a certain mental attitude and the discipline to follow an approach that exploits major long-term trends whenever they occur.

> The secret to a happy life is doing what you want and spending time with those who are important in your life. Analysing markets, evaluating strategies, and choosing investment classes and individual investments are time consuming. If you have the discipline to stick with a simple plan that works for you and your family, then self-directed investing will make sense for you.
>
> Harry S Dent Jr, author of *The Great Boom Ahead* and *The Roaring 2000s*

Develop a plan

As the saying goes, 'A failure to plan is a plan for failure' and never is that more true than when applied to investing. If you are unprepared, controlling your own investments can be an endeavour full of unpleasant surprises, and to avoid becoming sucked in by brokers, analysts, media spin or the euphoria of a speculative bubble you need to develop a game plan that enables you unemotionally to identify and exploit an investment trend. Those of you with prior market experience will no doubt develop and utilize your own strategies to exploit this bull market in commodities but it's not beyond the realm of novice investors also to harvest a profit if they follow a simple and straightforward investment strategy. No method is perfect because the markets are not perfect; however, if you can follow some of the strategies I use and have detailed in this book in a disciplined and rigorous manner, they will help you through the markets' ups and downs. If I'm correct in my beliefs about a tremendous appreciation in commodity values, then they will help you participate in the trend and not outstay your welcome at the end. In addition, operating this type of analysis should take you less than one hour a week.

If you are a newcomer, I think you will definitely benefit from understanding how my investment methods work and the disciplines they force upon you. I am not suggesting that my approaches are your only options, nor are they easy get-rich-quick solutions, but they will provide an investor and especially a novice investor with disciplines that have proved themselves profitable over many years. In addition, following such proven strategies offers some advantages as against a fundamental or discretionary investor trying to make the same decisions.

Firstly, rules-based investing makes life easier. What can be better than a profitable investment strategy that does not require your constant input? Just imagine, at the weekend you conduct your analysis, checking the market's performance. If there is a signal, you just place your order on the Monday morning and then it is off to work, the golf course, the gym, the shops, take the car for a spin, relax or whatever takes your fancy. This type of investing really does allow you the 'best of all worlds'!

Secondly, following a set of investment rules is better for you psychologically. A strategy containing the correct rules for investing provides you with the discipline required to succeed whilst also helping you avoid the mindless 'dabbling' that always costs investors money. To repeat, I believe successful investing is essentially more a test of someone's psychological strengths and weaknesses than a test of their intelligence or market knowledge. If you can understand and master the emotional pressures that investing can place you under, then that is far more important than understanding the laws of supply and demand or being able to dissect a company balance sheet.

Some academics argue that using 'a set of rules' to invest is not perfect, but as Larry Hite, an extremely successful fund manager and investment system designer, once said, 'It is incredible how rich you can get by not being perfect.'

How long-term investing works – disciplined trend following

> The sun never really goes down on investors who look for good value and invest along with powerful trends.
>
> Dan Denning, author of *The Bull Hunter*

'Trend following' is market terminology for any approach that concentrates on buying assets that are rising in price and selling assets that are falling in price. It is a price momentum-based strategy. Those who operate such an investment approach are usually looking to identify long-term 'trends' at an early stage of their development. They will then establish a position in the direction of that trend and 'follow it' by holding their position until the strategy they use indicates that the trend is over. Trend followers do not seek to anticipate how far a market is heading; they prefer to react to its most recent momentum. As a trend follower, I never set price targets or attempt to predict how far the market will move. Instead, I am just happy to sit and wait for the market to make its first moves and then jump on for the ride – just as surfers look to ride a good wave. They float in the sea looking for the physical signs that a strong wave is developing; then they prepare to jump on and ride it for as far as they can. They hope to have picked a wave with the power to carry them as far as possible, as quickly as possible and, if not, they will abort the run and look for another wave. Trend-following the markets is no different. If you catch a market with strong momentum, it could carry you a long way and produce fantastic profits. If not, jump off and wait for the next signal.

Why trend following works

All profitable systems trade trends; the difference in price necessary to create a profit implies a trend.

Ed Seykota

The main reason trend following works is because it imposes the correct disciplines that enable an investor to identify, participate in and remain with an investment trend. In addition, such a strategy is useful because it often identifies changes in the underlying fundamentals that affect long-term price movements before they have become common knowledge. The premise behind trend following is that the single most important piece of information about a market that any investor can utilize is the market price itself. Today's price is the sum total of the collective knowledge, hope, fear, greed and sentiment of all market participants. Fundamental analysis may point to higher or lower prices but the truth is that where the price is today is where everyone who has an opinion can buy or sell and it is also the marker by which their existing positions are showing a profit or a loss. Nothing else is as important. It therefore follows that any strategy that uses market prices to generate signals is going to be more thorough and more realistic than any other form of analysis.

The price of a market can never be 'too high' or 'too low'; it is just the price. One of my financial heroes is the highly respected market commentator, analyst and investor David Fuller, and I'm often reminded of his continual recommendation that when reviewing the price chart of any market we should just deal with the facts; everything else is conjecture. Where the price is today in relation to yesterday, last week, last month or last year is fact; whether it is going higher, lower or staying the same is pure conjecture.

Timing – do not predict, react

Trend following is a reactive process. To establish a position, we have to identify a trend before we can 'follow it' and then, to liquidate the same position, we need evidence that the market price has peaked and is now heading down. Being only reactive to recent price action means this type of analysis will never help you to invest at the lowest price or liquidate at the highest price but it will help you to hold on to a position for longer and often for a larger gain than the majority of market participants. It is no coincidence that the hedge funds and other alternative investment management companies that employ trend-following strategies are responsible for some of the most spectacular performance returns.

Trend-following strategies don't care whether prices are 'too high' or 'too expensive' or 'have rallied too far, too quickly'; they just follow the upward momentum of a trend.

Trend following is about being in the moment, basing your invest-ment decisions on fact – what is happening now in relation to the past. The future is not fact so don't bother worrying about it. Trend following is also simple to operate: if you invest in a market and in the future it continues rallying, you hold on to the position; if you invest in a market and it goes sideways, you hold on to the position; if you invest in a market and it goes down, you close your position. You don't know the future but you do know how a trend-following strategy will react to it.

Buy high to sell even higher

Although using a trend-following strategy is a simple mechanical process, actually responding to the signals such an approach provides can often be difficult for investors. Following upward price momentum means a trend follower will be investing in a market today that was or could have been considerably lower in price yesterday, last week or last month. This can be a hard concept to grasp because everybody loves a bargain. It's hard for most investors to purchase an asset for £60 today when last week it was worth £54, last month it was worth £41, and a year ago it was worth £32. If you operate a trend-following approach, you have to accept that you will always be investing today in an asset that in the recent past was relatively cheaper because it is the upward shift in prices that is actually generating the entry signal. Emotionally, you need to forget where prices have been because, if your investment is going to be profitable, prices aren't going back down there in the near future anyway. You need to stay focused on conducting your trend-following analysis and executing the signals as they're generated. To quote the highly successful, multibillion-dollar trend-following investment manager John W Henry, 'if you take emotion – would be, could be, should be – out of it, and look at what is, and quantify it, I think you have a big advantage over most human beings'.

Trend following means following trends, buying high to sell even higher. Don't let your emotions or the predictions of 'experts' distract you from this purpose.

Since I first began participating in the markets back in the 1980s, I have experimented with just about every method of analysis and time-frame available from fundamental to technical, from day-trading, where I held positions for no more than a couple of minutes, right up to long-term investment management, where positions were held for many years. For me, nothing has come close to matching the performance of a long-term trend-following strategy. It's easy to operate, helps you participate in the big investment trends and gets you out when they're over – maybe not the most intellectually stimulating way of investing but, personally speaking, definitely the most profitable and, after all, the purpose of investing your money is ultimately about just one thing: making more money.

Losers add to losers

Another beneficial aspect of adopting a trend-following strategy is that it helps you avoid one of the classic mistakes most investors make: adding to a losing position. A few years ago, I was chatting to a former fund manager and he related the following experience to me. He had decided to purchase the shares of a large British FTSE 100 quoted company, a UK 'household name'. The share price had fallen over 16 per cent from a recent peak of over £6 per share to £5 per share. He rationalized that the shares of this multibillion-pound company were now 'cheap' relative to its value a few months before. So he bought the shares at the 'bargain price' of approximately £5 per share. This purchase wasn't a particularly astute one as these shares eventually fell to below £2 before their slide had finished. So did he hold his position all the way down? Well, when they fell from his original purchase price to £4.25, he bought some more because they were 'even cheaper'. When the shares then fell to £3.50, he was sacked!

He learnt two very important lessons: 'Do not fight the trend' and 'In the markets, bad habits cost you money.' It does not matter how good the market is; it does not matter who the company is; it does not matter how strong the fundamental news is; if the price is weak, it is for a reason and you do not want to be involved. Most investors fall into the trap of buying just because the price is lower now than it was say six months ago. Everybody loves a bargain. However, this is a very dangerous investing tactic. Think: the market may be moving lower because something is seriously wrong and the reason behind the fall in price is not yet common knowledge to the investment community or the general public. This fund manager fell foul of the financial version of Russian roulette. No matter how many times one of your investments goes down in price and you increase your position and the market subsequently rallies back helping you achieve even more profit, you only need to be wrong once and this type of strategy could all but wipe you out! Adding to any investment position when its value is falling is like pulling the trigger on a gun. There might be four, five, six 'empty chamber clicks' and the market doesn't punish you for taking the risk but sooner or later you're destined to find the chamber with the bullet in it and then you're finished, period. The legendary 'market wizard' Paul Tudor Jones, for whom I was fortunate enough to manage money many years ago, had a poster on the wall of his office reminding him in bold letters: 'LOSERS AVERAGE LOSERS'. Thankfully, if you stick with a trend-following approach, adding to a losing position is not going to be a mistake you will ever make and there are far more interesting and profitable things you can do with your hard-earned cash than play financial Russian roulette.

Trend following vs buy and hold

You may wonder why it's so important to study the market to time your entries and exits. Why not just identify a potential investment and invest? In fact, there is a school of thought that believes it's impossible successfully to 'time' your investments and, instead, they recommend a strategy commonly known as 'buy and hold', which involves investing in the market from day one and sitting with the position until you either have reached a monetary target or need the money. Their premise is that over the long run you cannot predict the market's good days from the bad and, if you attempt to, then you will end up missing some of the best moves. So, by always remaining invested, you ensure that these strong price movements are never missed.

This appears to be a logical argument *but* – and this is a very important 'but' – although the theory sounds OK theorists generally do not make good investors and 'the buy and holders' miss an important point. As a buy and hold approach does not provide a disciplined exit rule, it offers no protection whatsoever against a market collapse, and those who adopt this type of investment strategy have to be prepared to sit through some scary market moves. That's when the emotional and the financial going gets really tough. As the highly successful billion-dollar systematic trend-following fund manager Jerry Parker remarked, 'The strategy of buy and hold is bad. Hold for what?'

Later in the book I will examine some well-known historical investment booms but, to illustrate just how a buy and hold strategy could trap you, let's quickly review two of them now. The first was in technology stocks, which saw the Nasdaq Composite Index (widely regarded as the barometer for these types of stocks) rally from 1,400 in September 1998 to over 5,000 by March 2000, before collapsing back down to 1,400 by September 2001. A buy and hold approach would have followed the market all the way up and then all the way back down again. The problem was even worse if you had been a buy and hold investor in the Japanese stock market when it had its boom in the late 1980s. The Nikkei 225 Index nearly reached 40,000 before collapsing over 80 per cent to below 8,000, and I know a couple of buy and hold investors who still need the Nikkei to rally nearly 400 per cent just to get their money back! If you think you would have closed your position to 'take some profits' or 'protect my gains' before the market collapsed, then you would not have been following the rules of a buy and hold strategy.

In contrast, a trend-following approach that times its entries and exits by generating signals based upon price movements can reduce risk by keeping investors out of the market during the downturns and then getting them back in during the rallies. Whilst it is possible that a buy and hold approach could generate bigger profits than trend following, these profits could come at a higher psychological price and it is a 'price' that I am not prepared to pay and neither should you.

To finish this chapter, I'd like to quote John W Henry again. Henry is one of the most successful investment managers in the world, controlling billions of dollars, with a performance record that places him at the top of his profession, and he's a committed trend follower: 'We can't always take advantage of a particular period. But in an uncertain world, perhaps the investment philosophy that makes the most sense, if you study the implications carefully, is trend following.'

3

The psychology of successful long-term investing

It's a mental game

To be a money master, you must first be a self-master.

JP Morgan

Before attempting to control your own investments you first need to make sure you're mentally prepared for the task, so let's now examine the psychological side of investing.

It is imperative you understand that keeping the psychological side of investing under control is going to be the key to a long and successful investment career. To help you further, let's have a look at some of the pressures that could trip you up in your journey as an investor. I recommend you read the following as many times as necessary to gain a full understanding.

The performance of most investment strategies is a good illustration of what is known as 'the 80/20 Principle' or 'Principle of Least Effort'. In 1897, the Italian economist Vilfredo Pareto made a fascinating discovery whilst studying the patterns of wealth and income in 19th-century England. He observed that a very small percentage of the population held a very large percentage of the wealth and, upon further study, also found that this imbalance was applicable to all manner of social and economic statistics. It would appear that a few citizens had obtained considerable wealth for very little effort, whilst the majority had worked extremely hard for very little reward, much the same as nowadays! Richard Koch's book *The 80/20 Principle* (see 'Further reading') covers the subject in great detail, and anyone who wishes to investigate the Principle of Least Effort further should obtain a copy. The 80/20 Principle is in our lives everywhere, far more than most people appreciate. Here are just a few examples of the imbalance in life:

- A minority of criminals will commit the majority of crimes.
- A minority of motorists will cause the majority of accidents.
- A minority of patients will have the majority of illnesses.
- You will wear a minority of your clothes the majority of the time.
- In sport, a minority of footballers will score the majority of goals.
- A minority of horses will win the majority of races.
- In a company, a minority of the employees will earn the majority of the wages.
- And a minority of the staff will have the majority of the sick leave!
- And so on…

More importantly, the 80/20 Principle is particularly evident in investing, where this imbalance leads to an inconsistency in the nature of equity returns, which in turn is one of the hardest psychological barriers to successful investing.

Let me explain.

There's no such thing as a steady return

The performance of any speculative financial, property or commodity investment will never provide an investor with consistent returns akin to a bank deposit account yield. This imbalance means investors should typically expect the majority of their profits to come from a minority of their investments, which additionally profit from only a very small percentage of the total time they are invested in a market. Investment profits are only achieved from upward price trends and, because the markets spend only a percentage of their time in such moves, it follows that the rest of the time they are not trending upwards and therefore profit opportunities remain limited. If, as an investor, you can accept that this will lead to an imbalance in returns, it will remove a great deal of the stress and pressure normally associated with speculating in the markets.

The 80/20 Principle illustrates that with the more speculative investments such as stocks and shares, property and commodities, there really is no such thing as an average return. However, it is easy to see how statistics can mislead. For example, let's examine the performance of the S&P 500 Composite Index (a broad-based measure for the United States stock market) for the 10-year period from 1990 to 1999. Over this period, the statistics show that the Index gained over 315 per cent, which is the equivalent of an average 15.31 per cent compounded annual return. However, if we examine the actual performance of each individual year (in percentages):

1990: −6.56	1995: +34.11
1991: +26.31	1996: +20.27
1992: +4.46	1997: +31.01
1993: +7.05	1998: +26.67
1994: −1.54	1999: +19.53

Source: www.standardandpoors.com

we can see that no single year showed an actual 15.31 per cent return. Some years were better but, more importantly, four years showed significantly lower returns than the average. This inconsistency of return does not make the stock market a bad investment but it does illustrate how unpredictable and volatile an investment can be even during a period of strong growth.

Accepting this inconsistency of return is psychologically important when you consider that the majority of the public are salaried employees and their experiences of earning money are normally in stark contrast to how investment profits are achieved. Employees are accustomed to a weekly or monthly wage without much variation in the amount of money received. Likewise, they will place a large percentage of their income into a bank or building society account and, whilst in most cases the cash will not stay in the account for very long, it will earn a consistent return from a fairly static interest rate. With their personal cash flow always conditioned to this uniform income, it often makes any investment venture they participate in a deeply unsettling one – to the degree that sooner or later most investors abandon an investment when it begins to display an inconsistency of return. Although everyone has different degrees of tolerance, unless you appreciate that your investment performance will be inconsistent you will eventually cry out. You must accept that imbalances exist in the distribution of returns and these may cause losing periods lasting several months before profits are achieved.

Get used to losing

The above heading may seem unusual but, as we have just reviewed, you will not and do not have to be correct all the time to profit as an investor. Successful investing is more about maximizing your profits when you're right rather than the number of times you are actually right. To illustrate the point, I've actually achieved my success by being wrong more times than I'm right. Yes, my win rate is lower than flipping a coin and such a strike rate can be very testing psychologically. For example, it has often been my unfortunate experience to establish a position in a market that has exhibited strong upward momentum in price only to see it turn and head in the opposite direction the day or week after I've bought. Also, there have been periods, some many months long, when I've not only failed to make an overall profit but also seem to have developed a talent for continually picking losers. If you decide to become an investor, it is highly likely that at some point in time you will also suffer this fate and, when you do, do not despair: losing is just a fact of investing life. Fortunately, the number of winning investments versus losing ones isn't that important. What really matters is how much profit you make when you're right compared to how much money you lose when you're wrong. When you win you want to win big, and when you lose you want to lose small.

This is a view confirmed by the successful billionaire investor George Soros, who once remarked, 'It doesn't matter how often you are right or wrong – it only matters how much you make when you are right, versus how much you lose when you are wrong.'

As an example, I might simultaneously hold four positions in different markets and, of these, three are losing £1,000 each whilst the fourth shows a £5,000 profit. Although my strike rate is only 25 per cent (one winner out of four positions), I'm still showing a total profit of £2,000 (£5,000 profit less £3,000 in total losses). When you adopt a trend-following strategy it is not unusual for this type of situation to occur but, providing you follow a strategy that forces you to run profitable positions whilst cutting the losers, you will still be successful in the long run. Of all the concepts involved in trend following and investing, I think this is the hardest one for the novice to grasp, and this isn't surprising when you think that nobody likes to be wrong. From our earliest memories as children, which are then reinforced throughout our school education, we are praised for being right and chastised for being wrong. If 'little Johnny' scores 10 out of 10 in his spelling test he gets a gold star. However, if he scores a measly 3 out of 10 it's considered a poor performance. With regard to our education and most careers, the number of times we're right versus wrong is an important measurement of our skill. I'm sure none of us would employ the services of an electrician who blew up 5 out of every 10 houses when rewiring. However, when it comes to investing, things are very different because the only true measurement of our skill is how much money we make. It's not how often your investments show a profit that matters; it is more important how much profit you make when you're right. Maximizing your profitable opportunities is, thankfully, something a trend-following strategy is usually very good at and, if you've got the discipline to stick with such an approach, you shouldn't do too badly. Leave your ego behind and focus less on the number of winners and losers you have and more on just sticking to your trend-following plan. It is a fallacy that a successful investor has to be correct all the time. I find it very easy to accept when I'm wrong. Participating in investments that don't work is something that happens to me all the time and I lose money on a regular basis because of this. However, the reason I'm still profitable despite these losers is that I can take these losses on the chin, wipe my mouth and move on. Then, when I participate in a profitable trend, I'm able to recover all those losses and achieve some serious profits. In fact, I've managed to do extremely well financially by being wrong at least as many times as I'm right. Lucky for some I didn't decide to become an electrician!

Discipline

It must be obvious to you by now that one of the most important attributes you will need in investing is 'discipline': the discipline to remain with your investment strategy regardless of what you may hear or read to the contrary; the discipline to remain invested when the markets enter the inevitable period when prices seem to be going nowhere, neither up nor down, and profits are minimal at best; and finally, when a bull market is rampant and every week you seem to be making more and more money, when your strategy finally indicates that you should liquidate your investment and cash in, that's when you'll need the discipline actually to instruct the broker to 'sell'. Often this is the toughest test and it's at this stage of the market cycle that I've seen many investors become greedy, abandoning their plan in order to squeeze a bit more profit from their investment, only to end up losing everything they have made. As I'll review later in the book, the final stage of a bull market is usually when everyone is talking about it and participating in it and the media are giving publicity to anyone who is making wild predictions of 'just how high prices could go'. It's easy during this euphoric stage for investors who have been in the trend for some time and are already flush with profits to become complacent, think they're also 'experts' and become carried away with what they read and hear, especially if it's predicting even greater profits for them. This is usually the time when investors lose their discipline and choose to ignore their strategies when instructed to close their positions. Investors choose to remain invested when they shouldn't be and eventually, when the trend finishes, it's usually with a sharp and dramatic retracement in prices that sends those who still hold positions into a kind of shock. Having already abandoned their plan and now without a clear strategy to guide them, they become mentally paralysed, as they can't believe what's happening to their investment and the profits they once had. Stuck like rabbits in car headlights they often take to staring at their market quote machines, market data websites or the financial television channels in disbelief, hoping and praying that prices will recover to their previous levels so they can close their positions without too much damage. Well, in the early stages of my career I've been in just such a situation and I can assure you that neither hope nor prayer works. The upshot of all this market volatility and mental turmoil is that those investors who either had no investment plan or abandoned the one they had because they became greedy are usually destined to remain invested as the market retraces its previous rally all the way back down. You might think you wouldn't be so undisciplined and stupid. Well, I hope you're not, but many are, and even some professionals get caught in this emotional and financial roller coaster. Also, as we will shortly review, it is not uncommon for markets to behave in this way, so you do need to be prepared.

Temperament

> The difference between a successful person and others is not a lack of strength, not a lack of knowledge, but rather a lack of will.
>
> Vince Lombardi

If you decide to control your own investments, you need to be 'professional' in your approach and possess the correct temperament. The dictionary defines temperament as 'manner of thinking or behaving of a particular individual'. The correct temperament for successful investors demands they see things as they are and can evaluate everything with cold, unemotional logic. There is no room for impulsiveness, no room for fads or fancies and no room for high elation with success or sickening gut feelings when things go wrong. It follows that you have no time for chopping or changing your investment approach but must proceed in a disciplined and methodical manner. You must remain focused and ignore advice to the contrary. Just because a supposedly knowledgeable person makes a statement, it does not necessarily follow that it is correct. Any opinion that has even the remotest personal connection will almost inevitably carry a bias and is therefore suspect. You must learn to evaluate everything completely devoid of sentiment and maintain confidence in the ability of the investment strategy you have chosen. Start to invest, instead of gambling. Do not allow yourself to make 'little side bets' following analyst tips, media gossip or 'something I heard down the pub'.

In summary, you're probably now well aware that I consider long-term investing to be primarily a 'mind game'. In fact you will often find that the only difference in performance between two virtually identical investors holding the same views will be down to how they control themselves mentally during the ups and downs of the market. Investing is more a test of your 'EQ' (emotional intelligence) than your 'IQ', and the best way to ensure you can cope with the psychological pressure is to have a plan and to stick to it. Don't attempt to be the best, just the most balanced and disciplined.

4

Financing your investments

Perception of risk

This ain't clipping coupons. No risk, no return.

Anonymous

Risk, or more importantly your own perception of risk, is a key factor in deciding whether you will become an investor, let alone how much of your hard-earned cash you're prepared to commit. Because the focus of this book is based upon the potential for a boom in commodity prices, your own perception of whether commodities are a risky investment or not is going to play a major part in you deciding if you're going to participate in them. Although commodities can be extremely volatile, a recent study by the Yale International Center for Finance, which I will examine in more detail later in the book, illustrated that over the last 40 years commodities have, in fact, been no more volatile than the stock market whilst actually achieving greater returns. However, despite this evidence many will still regard commodities to be a riskier investment. This is because, when it comes to making decisions where we perceive an element of risk, we like to think we are pragmatic and grounded individuals, but often it's our emotions that take over and, as John Nofsinger writes in his book *Investment Madness* (see 'Further reading'), 'your own psychological biases can creep into your investment decisions and sabotage your attempts at building wealth'.

In short, we humans tend to perceive risk primarily as an emotional deduction and, even though this is not necessarily a deliberate thought process, it is the way evolution has wired our brains. This misconception is applicable in all areas of our lives and often results in incorrect and illogical conclusions. For example, I have a friend who smokes 40 cigarettes a day and yet refuses to use a mobile phone because he fears it will cause cancer. Current figures show that last year over 120,000 people died in Britain as a direct result of smoking, whilst it's yet to be proven that one single person has died from using a mobile phone. Similarly, one of my relatives spends most of the working week driving up and down the motorway yet refuses even to consider flying because it is too dangerous. Now, statistically both of these people are 'backing the wrong horse' because it is their perception of risk rather than the statistical evidence that influences their opinions.

Misconceptions exist in abundance in the world of investing. For instance, the general public are now heavily investing in property, as they consider it to be a far safer and more profitable investment than any other. However, just over 10 years ago, when property values were falling and 'negative equity' was rife, there were thousands bankrupted by their property investments. Nobody seems to recall this tragedy or, if they do, we get the 'this time around it's different' answer.

> The four most dangerous words in investing are 'It's different this time.'
>
> The legendary investor Sir John Templeton

Time seems to heal and again perception rules over our investment decisions. There are also many who now consider both stocks and property to be too risky and instead are content to keep their money in a bank deposit account earning less than 3 per cent a year. Commodity prices do not have to appreciate that much before higher inflation returns and when that happens the real value of a bank or building society account balance will start to go down. Nothing is completely risk free and sometimes, even if you think you are not risking anything, you are wrong.

> There are risks and costs to a program of action. But they are far less than the long-range risks and costs of comfortable inaction.
>
> John F Kennedy

Your financial commitment

Assuming you're still with me and prepared to accept an element of risk for the right return, let's now get down to the nitty-gritty of financing your investments. Any business endeavour, including investing, needs to be well capitalized to be successful, and deciding upon how much money you can afford to allocate is one of the most important and influential investment decisions you will ever make. The larger the amount you can comfortably commit and the sooner you can do it, the likelier it is to result in tremendous changes to your future. This is because the key to the amount of profit you can achieve from most investments largely depends upon the amount of money you invest and the length of time it is invested for. The larger the initial investment and the longer the investment time-frame, the greater the monetary returns you will achieve.

However, before deciding upon the size of your financial commitment, you need to consider what you are aiming to achieve from investing. What are your financial goals – clearing credit cards, funding the education of your children, starting a business venture, paying off the mortgage on your home, funding your retirement etc? Whatever you decide your financial goals are, make sure they are not unrealistic relative to the size of the capital you have available to invest. There is no point in saying you want to fund your retirement in 10 years time if you have only got £500 to invest. Long-term investing via a trend-following strategy is good, but to achieve a goal like that you would need a miracle.

One of the biggest mistakes investors can make is setting unrealistic goals and putting too much pressure on themselves to perform. To give you an example, a few years ago following a speaking engagement at an investment seminar a member of the audience approached me. He explained that he wanted to take his family to Disneyland the following year and pay for the holiday from his investing profits. He said the holiday was going to cost around £1,500 and he had about £300 to invest; did I know of any leveraged investment that could help him turn his £300 into £1,500 in the next six months? This guy was seriously attempting to make a 400 per cent return in just six months and, whilst some investors occasionally get lucky with a 'hot tip', there was no way on God's earth this was a realistic strategy. In fact, if I were a betting man I would wager that he would have lost all of his investment cash way before the six months was up! Thankfully, I was able to get him to rethink his plan. Unrealistic goals not only place investors under tremendous psychological pressures, but they also play a major part in them abandoning competent strategies simply because they were expecting too much from them. You do not set unrealistic goals in other areas of your life, such as learning to drive a car and passing your driving test in a day or going on a diet aiming to lose four stones in one week, so why do it with your investments? For long-term success, your financial goals need to be realistic and achievable.

Although trend following is a great strategy for profiting from powerful bull markets, it does not provide immunity from losses, and there will be occasions in the future when it will hit the inevitable losing run. It is at this point that your true commitment will be tested. If you have set unrealistic goals and invested too aggressively relative to your lifestyle, net worth and emotional risk tolerance, using cash that you cannot afford to leave for a long period of time, then a losing run will cause you unnecessary stress and usually results in you abandoning your plan. 'Sod's Law' then normally rears its ugly head and you can bet that the next signal, which you do not act upon because you have suffered too much pain already, turns out to be the biggest winner of the decade!

Structuring your commitment

Let's now look at how much you can invest. Because everybody is different and we all have differing incomes, lifestyles and financial goals, it's impossible for me to recommend a specific initial investment amount. However, I would suggest you only invest money that you have no immediate plans for. By 'immediate', I mean cash that can be left alone for at least three to four years. If you do not have such money available as investment capital, then you need to get it quickly. Save; delay buying that new car; give up smoking etc – whatever. It is important to begin your investment career as soon as possible. However, *do not* borrow the cash. Although at the time of going to press interest rates were at their lowest levels for decades, I do not recommend borrowing money to invest. One very important attribute an investor needs to possess is 'patience', the patience to leave your capital to work in the markets. There will be times in the future when the markets appear to lack direction and remain in an unexciting sideways movement and this is when your resolve may well be tested. If you have borrowed money to invest, then having to make monthly interest payments on the debt without seeing any profit from the market may be too much of a financial and emotional strain. Your long-term investments need to be treated exactly the same as a pension contribution, which is normally left to grow until such time as you are allowed access. Although you can access your investment cash almost immediately, I would prefer you to treat it as if you cannot. To keep it separate on the occasions when you don't have any investment positions, I recommend you open an instant access savings account into which you can transfer the cash and earn some interest; then when you have identified a new entry signal you can simply transfer the cash back to the broker whenever it is required. Additionally you should make sure this account is opened with a different bank or building society to the one you normally use. This is to avoid the temptation of dipping into your investment capital. Under no circumstances should you transfer the cash back into your everyday banking accounts. Keeping the money separate is important because the longer you can remain committed to leaving your investment cash untouched, the greater its chances of appreciating.

Asset allocation

Deciding how much of your money you're going to place into a partic-ular investment or asset class falls under the impressive-sounding title of 'asset allocation'. It's an important part of the investing process and it can actually make the difference between spectacular long-term successes and just mediocre returns. Normally the first word that pops into most advisers' and investors' heads when the subject of asset allocation comes up is 'diversification'. They tend to think in terms of spreading risk across a broad and diverse group of different asset classes. This should ensure that, if any one particular asset class underperformed, your losses could be offset by another better-per-forming investment and, because nobody knows in advance which are going to be the best-performing assets, the prudent step is usually to balance out your investment cash across a mix of safe and slightly risky asset classes. The safer an investment is perceived to be, usually the larger the amount of money that is invested, whilst the more speculative assets will receive smaller chunks of your cash. A 'typical' portfolio might look something like this:

Fixed income bonds	30 per cent allocation
Long-term bank deposit	50 per cent allocation
Stock market investment	15 per cent allocation
Offshore hedge fund	5 per cent allocation

I am not going to criticize anyone for recommending or following such an allocation of funds because, for the majority of people, investing their hard-earned cash is a scary experience fraught with uncertainty and risk. The only problem with adopting such a strategy is that it doesn't offer you much potential for earning exceptional profits. Remaining invested in underperforming assets simply because they offer diversification is going to provide you with poor returns that may, after advisory fees, actually underperform inflation. This could mean that in 'real' terms you're actually losing money. Referring to the above portfolio, let's suppose that the stock market re-entered a bull market phase of similar magnitude to the one that occurred in the 1990s, and there's no reason why that couldn't happen again. If you keep your money rigidly allocated as in our 'typical' portfolio example, only a small percentage of your funds will be participating in the move and, because a stock market rally could partly be the result of a decline in interest rates, it's also quite possible that any gains your portfolio enjoys from the stock market allocation will be undermined by the portfolio's continued participation in the now underperforming interest rate-based investments. This doesn't mean following such a path will lose you money but you will definitely not make as much as you could have. You and your portfolio will underachieve.

A dynamic approach

I personally favour a slightly different approach to asset allocation, one that involves concentrating your current investments in asset classes and/or markets that are appreciating in value until such time as they lose this momentum; then I get out and wait for the next investment opportunity. It doesn't matter to me whether I'm invested in stocks, bonds, property or commodities; as long as the trend-following methods I'm using still indicate that prices are moving up, then I want to be invested. Operating a trend-following strategy will identify these investments, it will help you monitor them and then it will signal when to liquidate. In my view, correct asset allocation is about concentrating your cash in assets that are significantly appreciating in value and avoiding everything else. You're trying to be in the right place at the right time. Nothing else matters.

If I'm concentrating on just one asset class, which is usually the case, I often use an asset allocation strategy that involves dividing my capital into five equal amounts. I then monitor with my trend-following methods every related market or investment vehicle in that asset class, acting upon any entry signals generated until I'm participating in five of them and therefore fully invested. For example, let's suppose I was bullish on global stocks and shares. I would apply my analysis across a number of different countries' stock indices and as each one generated an entry signal I would then respectively invest one-fifth (20 per cent) of my investment capital. Assuming I was correct in my original analysis and global stocks entered a bull market, I would eventually be fully invested in stocks and shares across five strong-performing markets. For another example, let's look at where I think the next big investment opportunity is going to be – commodities. Having already decided this is where I want my cash invested, I participate as follows. Conducting my weekly analysis on all the major commodity markets, I will invest in the first five markets that generate an entry signal as defined by the methods detailed later in the book and invest an equal 20 per cent of my investment capital in each. Although all my capital will be committed to a single asset class, I'm increasing my chances of catching a big winner by dividing my investment across five different commodities at any one time. If one market generates an exit signal, I close this position and then wait for my weekly analysis to provide the next new entry signal upon which I will act, adding this new market to my portfolio. This type of asset allocation strategy isn't diversifying my risk but that is not its intention. Instead, I just want to increase my chances of participating in the leading commodity trends whenever they occur. This is particularly important when you consider that even in a global commodity boom not all the individual commodity markets will appreciate together. An excellent example of this fractured market behaviour occurred during the last commodity boom back in the 1970s. During this period, soybean prices went through the roof in 1972; sugar had its massive bull market two years later in 1974; coffee's bull market began in 1976; whilst gold and silver didn't really get going until the end of the decade.

Although this asset allocation strategy may seem a little basic, it would have performed admirably in the 1970s boom and it shouldn't do too badly in the next one either. Granted, things may be a little different this time around, but let's not forget that price momentum is the real driver for investing, and my methods should ensure I'm only participating in markets that are moving upwards.

To recap, here is my recommended asset allocation strategy:

1. Divide your total investment cash into five equal amounts (eg £20,000 divided by 5 = £4,000).
2. Following an entry signal, commit one of these amounts to the respective market (eg entry signal generated in copper = invest £4,000 in copper).
3. When you have acted upon five signals and hold positions in five different markets, you are now fully invested and should ignore any new entry signals from other markets for the time being.
4. When you receive an exit signal for a market in which you hold a position, close the position and bank the cash. You are now free to accept the next entry signal whenever it is generated.

As the individual commodity markets move through their own mini-cycles, you will find the composition of your portfolio will change. For example, as I write this text my current investment portfolio consists of positions in copper, crude oil, gold, soybeans and unleaded gasoline. Yet four months ago, it consisted of cocoa, coffee, cotton, crude oil and silver. This strategy is not sophisticated but it helps to concentrate cash in assets that are appreciating in value. To me that's common sense.

Compounding

> Those who understand compound interest are destined to collect it.
> Those who don't are doomed to pay it.

> Tom and David Gardner, The Motley Fools

As I stated earlier, it is widely recognized that there are two key elements to the degree of success you will attain from your investments: firstly, the size of the initial investment – the larger the better; and, secondly, the amount of time it is invested over – the longer the better. Compounding will do the rest.

Once described by Albert Einstein as 'the eighth wonder of the world' and without a doubt the financial world's best-kept secret, compounding is actually a very simple concept. Basically, if an investment appreciates by a similar percentage each year, the actual monetary value of each respective annual increase becomes larger. The effect on the growth of the cash is known as 'compounding'. To illustrate, if you had invested £10,000 and this appreciated by 10 per cent per annum, then the actual monetary gain for the first year would be £1,000 (10 per cent of £10,000). However, an equal 10 per cent gain the next year equates to a monetary gain of £1,100 (10 per cent of £11,000). Because the first year profit has been reinvested, the annual percentage gain is on a larger capital figure. This is compounding at work. If you could achieve a 10 per cent gain every year and continued to reinvest the profit, then through the benefit of compounding the £10,000 investment would have doubled in less than eight years. If you had withdrawn each annual profit, then it would have taken an extra two years to achieve the same result. The effect of compounding means a fixed percentage gain reinvested produces an exponential monetary gain.

The seriously rich love to play the compounding game and it is no coincidence that they primarily invest in asset classes that benefit from it. One of those asset classes is property and in the past few years most homeowners will have experienced the benefits of compounding. To illustrate, let's look at a couple who bought their home in the 1960s for approximately £3,000. By 2000, its value could easily have been in excess of £300,000 and, whereas a 10 per cent gain in house prices in 1961 would have meant a monetary gain of £300, exactly the same percentage increase in 2001 would have equated to a monetary gain of

£30,000. One year's appreciation in value in 2001 was equal to 10 times the original cost of the house! This is compounding at work and there is an interesting algorithm that not only illustrates its power but also serves as a useful guide for calculating its effect on your investments. It is known as the 'Rule of 72'.

Rule of 72

The Rule is easy to understand and operate. Essentially, you divide your expected annual percentage gain into 72. The answer then equates to the number of years it will take your investment to double in value. For example, if your investment grows at an annual rate of 10 per cent, then it will take 7.2 years for the investment to double in value (72 divided by 10 = 7.2); if the investment grows at a rate of 15 per cent per annum, then it will take 4.8 years for it to double (72 divided by 15 = 4.8). Although an annual percentage gain is usually educated guesswork, the Rule of 72 provides a good illustration of how minor increases in an annual rate of return can have a dramatic effect on an investment's long-term performance. In summary, the longer an investment is left to compound the greater its effect on the performance of the investment.

Leverage

It is possible to increase the effect of compounding even more if you apply leverage to your investment cash. If compounding is like a high-performance engine that drives your investments forward, then leverage acts like a turbo, providing even greater acceleration. However, leverage can also be very dangerous, if not controlled.

The most common form of financial leverage encountered in every-day life is when we use a loan to purchase something. The purchase of a home is a good illustration of leverage at work. Most lenders will advance at least 80 per cent of the purchase price of a property as a mortgage. Therefore, a cash amount of £20,000 could buy a property worth £100,000. This is leverage. If the value of the property increases by 10 per cent over the next year, then it will be worth £110,000 (£100,000 + £10,000 annual gain) but this increase of £10,000 represents a 50 per cent gain on the original £20,000 cash investment! Obtaining an asset worth £100,000 with a £20,000 personal investment equates to a leverage factor of five to one, which means that every 1 per cent movement in the value of an asset represents a fivefold move on the underlying cash investment. Whilst this all sounds great if values are rising, the opposite is true if your investment begins to depreciate, and that is why the following warning is so important:

Wealth warning: Leverage can seriously damage your wealth.

Trend-following investment strategies can benefit from the application of leverage but, because they're also subject to the occasional losing period, you must never use a disproportionately high level of leverage relative to your investment capital. To be used wisely, leverage needs to be restricted and, if you decide to use it, I recommend you limit it to no more than a maximum of two times the cash amount you have decided to invest. This means you multiply the cash by no more than a leverage factor of two to one. For example, a cash investment of £3,000 would mean your leveraged investment amount should be no greater than £6,000 (£3,000 × 2). This degree of leverage is still large and means a 20 per cent movement in an asset will actually be the equivalent of a 40 per cent gain or loss on the money you have invested. Leverage is an aggressive way of trying to boost your investment returns and it is definitely not a suitable strategy for the inexperienced investor.

The choice of whether or not to leverage your cash has to be a personal one and under no circumstances should you feel pressured to apply it to your investments. I can assure you that, even if you have only the bare minimum to invest and just follow a sound trend-following investment strategy without any form of leverage, you'll still be amazed at how quickly even a small initial investment can grow. In addition, you can always consider contributing more money to your investment pot if and when you receive an annual bonus or other windfall gain.

5

Developing an investment strategy

Your next task is to develop your own investment strategy. But before we look at the various methods I use and want you to consider incorporating into your own personal investment analysis, let's examine the core ingredient from which all profits and losses are achieved, the long-term investment trend.

The profile of an investment boom

All economic movements by their very nature are motivated by crowd psychology.

Bernard Baruch

With regard to investment trends and speculative bubbles, history does indeed repeat itself and we can learn a great deal from examining how past booms began, accelerated and then ended. Although we like to think of ourselves as more intelligent, rational, wise, sophisticated and educated than our predecessors, we are in fact no different when it comes to investing. This is because, like it or not, most investors base their investment decisions upon their emotions. It makes no difference whether the investment trend is driven by unsound fundamentals because if prices appreciate fast enough sooner or later the trend will be hijacked by the mass emotional drivers of 'fear' and 'greed'. At this stage, regardless of any fundamental evidence to the contrary, it will be the investment community's current mood that will decide whether the trend continues or falters. This is not a new phenomenon and, to prove it, the most widely accepted study on the subject is a book published over 160 years ago in 1841. Such is the appeal of *Extraordinary Popular Delusions and the Madness of Crowds* by Charles Mackay (see 'Further reading') that it's still in print today and remains a fascinating read for anyone who wishes to explore further the subject of crowd psychology.

As I have already repeated on many occasions in this book and will continue to do so, I believe the psychology of investing is more important than any other aspect of the business. Having already dealt with its application to the individual investor I now want to concentrate on the psychology of an investment 'crowd' and how it affects an investment trend. If we can identify some commonality between investment trends, then it is possible to profit from knowing where we are in the current investment cycle, whether it is still a good time to invest and also how much further the trend could continue.

From an analytical perspective, I believe all major investment trends can be broken down into three stages:

■ *Stage one – Prices have gradually begun to rise but not sufficiently for most people to take an interest.* This first stage is the most profitable time to invest but usually very few people, including many professionals, are aware or even interested that values have begun to rise and, except for a few insiders who are already making profits, the vast majority of investors, the media and the public are just not interested.

■ *Stage two – Prices have begun to move higher, leaving behind the lower values of the stage one period.* At this stage of a bull market cycle, everybody is aware that prices have risen and are continuing to rise but many believe that values are already too high. A 'market has gone too far too quickly' mentality illustrates that, although many are now interested in participating, they haven't yet done so because the mood of the crowd is not yet euphoric. Everyone loves a bargain and it's a difficult decision for most investors now to participate in an asset or invest in a market that only a few weeks or months ago was relatively cheaper.

■ *Stage three – Prices are accelerating higher and developing an exponential curve.* At this stage of the cycle, with momentum so strong, this 'new' bull market is the topic at every dinner party, it is on the cover of every finance magazine, bookshops are full of new titles written by 'experts' and even your doctor, dentist or dustman has become an authority on the subject and proudly announces a change of career to become a full-time speculator. You might remember the stories of many folk leaving their mundane jobs to become full-time 'day-traders' during the most recent boom in tech stocks. Stage three is the end, maybe not immediately and prices may rise a lot further, but sooner or later it is the end and, as is the way with all boom/ bust cycles, it's those who were least prepared at the beginning and now most committed at the end who will suffer the greatest.

Historical comparisons

Time and again we can avoid disastrous pitfalls and learn to profit by seeing the ways that history repeats itself.

Charles Mackay, author of *Extraordinary Popular Delusions and the Madness of Crowds*

To give you a taste of just how irrational investors can be and also to illustrate the three stages every boom undergoes as it evolves, I want briefly to review some famous examples of past investment booms.

The Dutch Tulip Mania, 1634–37

It's hard to believe that the first accurately recorded major investment boom involved tulip bulbs but maybe this isn't so surprising when you consider that the Dutch Tulip Mania occurred during the same period in history that thousands of innocent women, including midwives, were burnt at the stake as witches. Back in the 17th century the tulip was a highly prized commodity. In fact, to own one was considered the ultimate status symbol, a possession only available to the upper classes similar to owning a yacht or helicopter nowadays. Originating from Turkey, tulips (the name derived from the Turkish word for 'turban') entered Europe in the mid-16th century via Constantinople. They immediately proved popular in both Germany and Holland where connoisseurs would marvel at their beautiful, vivid colours. As with most plants that grow from a bulb, tulips produce the same colour flower each year but unusually some varieties of tulip would 'break' their colouring pattern displaying an eye-catching striped change in colour. Although these colour changes were the result of a virus, such was their beauty that these unusual blooms developed into a highly collectable commodity and, whereas collectors of antique furniture or other decorative artefacts were required to pay fortunes to increase their collections, the owner of a highly prized tulip merely had to let nature take its course each year at no extra cost. The attraction of owning a tulip as an investment in the 17th century was twofold in that they were highly collectable at a high retail price and they multiplied annually at little cost to the producer, similar to owning a rare breed of animal and selling its offspring each year. The much-sought-after 'freak' tulips were categorized into three groups: the 'bizarden' (red or violet on a yellow background), the 'roses' (red and pink on a white background) and the 'violets' (lilac and purple on a white background). They were named after famous figures of the day and it was considered a sign of improper breeding not to own at least one such variety of tulip. Just as the newly affluent of this day and age are eager to flaunt their status with big cars, big houses and exotic holidays, so it was over 370 years ago, only the status symbol was different – it was a flower. Demand swiftly 'outgrew' supply, if you will excuse the pun, and to meet this increased demand tulip producers worked on growing even more colourful strains. By 1612 there were over a hundred varieties sold in Amsterdam alone. Even the royal families of Europe participated, such were the appeal and kudos associated with owning an exotic tulip. Producers also began to grow tulip varieties that fell within the reach of the smaller buyer, and one of the most popular was 'Semper Augustus', a red and white striped flower with a blue-tinted base (the colours incorporated in the national flag of the Netherlands). In 1623, the renowned 'tulip expert' Wassenauer noted that 'one has been sold for thousands of florins; yet the seller himself was sold, for when the bulb was lifted he noticed two lumps on it which the year following would have become two offsets, and so he was cheated of 2,000 florins – interest, while the capital remains'.

Up until the 1630s, tulip investing had primarily remained the domain of the gentry but, as producers grew smaller, more affordable varieties, so the entry cost lowered and more citizens began to participate. Even the lower classes entered into the market, buying small amounts of tulips so as to be able to boast to their neighbours. It was even recorded that children starved as parents used their income to buy tulips instead of food. The boom was now well and truly under way. For just a small investment a citizen could benefit from the appreciation of a tulip and earn profits that way exceeded their hard-earned wages. Even the most common varieties were quickly appreciating in price. For example, a 40-florin 'Centen' bulb saw its price rally over 700 per cent to 350 florins in just two years, and the 'Admiral de Maan' tulip went from 15 florins to 175 florins, a 1,000 per cent plus rise over the same period. Prices for the rarer varieties also went through the roof, with one bulb sold for 4,600 florins plus a new carriage and two horses. However, at the height of the mania, this same variety of bulb sold for over 6,000 florins. To give you a marker, at the same time you could buy cattle for 100 florins.

By the mid-1630s, everyone was talking about and investing in tulips. They were sold in every village and town and yet demand still outstripped supply. Also, owing to the constraints of the growing season, it was now possible to purchase your tulip bulb before it had even been grown, thereby creating a kind of tulip futures market. By the spring of 1637, when speculation reached its height, buyers and sellers were investing in nothing more than pieces of paper bearing notional delivery dates. You didn't even need money, as many sellers would accept anything in payment. In one recorded example, a 'Viceroy' bulb was sold in exchange for the following: four barrels of beer, two barrels of butter, 12 fat sheep, four fat oxen, two loads of wheat, eight fat pigs, four loads of rye, 1,000 pounds of cheese, a suit of clothes, a silver beaker and a bed. At times like this, when people are investing everything they own to participate in an investment that has already grown many-fold and it's the topic on everyone's lips, then it's stage three of the investment cycle – the end. And so it was with the Dutch Tulip Mania – on 4 February 1637, to be precise. The catalyst is vague but rumour had it that a few growers became worried about a potential default and decided to liquidate their business. Their selling caused prices to fall, which in turn concerned other producers and, to protect themselves from further profit erosion, they also decided to sell. The knock-on effect had begun and prices fell like a stone. In fact, within just one week, the price of a tulip was close to zero and you couldn't give them away. Thousands of people, the rich, the middle class and the poor, were bankrupted.

Although this investment bubble was unusual in that it was based purely upon a commodity that had nothing more than a perceived 'status symbol' value, it still exhibited all the classic ingredients we can expect from a strong investment trend. To recap, during stage one of the cycle between 1620 and 1630, prices appreciated at a steady but relatively unspectacular rate; then in stage two of the cycle, between 1631 and 1635, prices moved higher relatively faster until they rallied exponentially as tulip prices entered stage three of their cycle between 1636 and early 1637. The end when it came was swift and painful but the warning signs had been there for many months before and as we will see in later investment booms, it will only be those investors who can ignore the hype at the height of a trend and remain focused, who will survive.

The South Sea Bubble, 1719–20

The next major investment boom I want to review occurred during the early 18th century. At this point in history, the City of London had three great financial institutions: the Bank of England, the East India Company and the South Sea Company. The latter was founded on 3 May 1711 when the House of Commons passed a resolution establishing the 'Governor and Company of the merchants of Great Britain, trading to the South Seas and other parts of America and for the encouragement of fishing'. The venture was designed to bring wealth to its investors but unfortunately the undisciplined majority suffered terrible financial losses in what became known as 'the South Sea Bubble'.

Back in the early 18th century, for the first time in over 200 years Britain had an opportunity to gain access to the commodities of South America, which had previously been under the monopoly of Spain. With the War of the Spanish Succession nearing a conclusion and thanks to the efforts of the Duke of Marlborough, there was now a prospect for Britain to make inroads into this lucrative market. The newly formed South Sea Company would be granted exclusive rights to trade with the eastern edge of South America, from the Orinoco River in Venezuela to Tierra del Fuego on the southern tip of Argentina, and along the whole of the western coast. Whilst providing British merchants with the opportunity to open new trade in a distant and hitherto inaccessible continent, the company was also intended to bail out the British government from its national debt crisis.

The War of the Spanish Succession ended in 1713 with the Treaty of Utrecht and, despite the Duke of Marlborough's notable victories, Britain did not benefit as well as it had hoped from the treaty. In addition to picking up Nova Scotia, Minorca and a bit of rock that's still a thorn in the Spanish flesh called Gibraltar, it received precious little in the way of trade contracts. In fact Britain was allowed just one ship per year to trade with Chile, Mexico or Peru – not exactly a windfall, but this didn't stop representatives from the South Sea Company from claiming a major economic coup. An 18th-century public relations exercise had swung into action and it didn't take long to convince the general public that this was a major investment opportunity. In 1720, the South Sea Company began offering its shares to the public. However, the money raised did not go directly to the company but instead was handed to the British government to reduce an ever-increasing national debt. In return, the government had agreed to grant the South Sea Company commercial privileges. When the latter information was made public following Parliament's formal acceptance on 2 February 1720, the value of the company's shares rose immediately. In that month alone, they rallied 42 per cent from £129 to £184 and more than doubled again in March to £380. This gain of nearly 200 per cent in just two months captured the imagination of the public. Here was an investment appreciating at a phenomenal rate, sanctioned by the British government, publicly supported by the royal family, Members of Parliament and noblemen from both sides of the English Channel. And what's more, there was a special investment condition that enabled an investor to purchase shares for just a 20 per cent down payment with the balance payable in monthly instalments thereafter. Not only did this special purchase deal enable the less well-off to participate, but it also allowed those with more capital to leverage their investments aggressively.

With a non-stop barrage of outrageously positive announcements released to a greedy and gullible audience, demand for South Sea

Company shares soared. One press release even claimed that the Spanish in Mexico were prepared to exchange their gold for a collection of colourful ponchos, such was their desire to trade with Britain. The public believed every word and greedily risked their entire livelihoods investing in the company. By May 1720, its shares had rallied to £500 and then rocketed again to £800 during the first week of June. They peaked on 24 June, at £1,050, which represented a gain of 700 per cent in just over 19 weeks. In addition, the success of the South Sea Company stock had also inspired other entrepreneurs to set up their own companies and it wasn't long before a number of these were quoted on the exchange. As this investment mania reached its peak in the summer of 1720, there were hundreds of these investment companies in existence and, as the desperation of both businessmen and investors to jump on this bandwagon increased, so the more outrageous their business plans became. For example, companies were launched to trade in human hair; extract silver from lead; cure broken-winded horses; maintain bastard children; transmutate animals; discover the secret of perpetual motion; fire square cannonballs; and, finally, cure lunacy, which considering how mad everyone had become with their investing probably wasn't such a bad idea. The best illustration of how out of control this investment boom had now become came from a shady entrepreneur who decided to sell shares in 'a company for carrying on an undertaking of great advantage, but nobody to know what it is'. The prospectus guaranteed an annual return of £100 for every £2 share purchased. You may have thought investors would have been wary of investing their cash into a business that promised an unbelievable 5,000 per cent annual return whilst not revealing any information whatsoever about how these returns would be generated. In a sane, rational environment, they may have asked some questions, but this was stage three of the investment cycle, a time when all normally sensible and cautious individuals leave their brains in a box under the stairs and believe literally everything they're told, no matter how outrageous. Such was the greed of the investment crowd that this particular company's shares were sold out on the morning of the first day. Needless to say, this was the last time its investors saw their money. This type of mindless buying frenzy is the hallmark of a stage three ending.

The end for the South Sea Bubble when it came on 24 June 1720 was, as is the case with all the really powerful investment trends, swift and painful. However, had investors acted quickly once prices began to fall, many would still have been able to liquidate their investments for a profit. Unfortunately, greed once again took over. Having seen the South Sea stock trade at over £1,000, the vast majority could not now bring themselves to sell at £810, which is where prices had retreated by mid-August. This is a classic mistake and, as we will see, it's a mistake that has been repeated in every investment boom throughout history. Without a plan or strategy, investors make all their decisions based upon their emotions. What tends to happen in these situations is, as the market moves ever higher, investors become accustomed to every new high price; constantly calculate how much their investment is worth and the amount of profit they've achieved, dreaming about how they will spend their new-found wealth. Then, all of a sudden, prices fall. Disbelief is normally the first emotion, followed by a stubborn reluctance to accept the game has now changed. It's often at this point that undisciplined investors who still have some spare cash available use it to increase their investment at this 'cheap, bargain price'. If the price falls further, many will invest even more until they have no spare capital left. This type of behaviour is surprisingly common as investments begin to retrace a previously strong up-trend. As a trend follower, I personally can see no logical reason or justification for investing in an asset that is falling in price from an already extreme level. In the long run, adopting such a tactic is financial suicide; even if an investor gets lucky and the price rallies, adopting this type of blind faith approach means you only need to be wrong once to get wiped out!

The only way to deal with an emotionally testing situation such as the end of an investment trend is to have a strategy that forces you to liquidate when prices fall. When a market turns, your first priority is to protect as much of your capital and outstanding profits as possible and the only way to achieve this is to close your investment position immediately.

Back in the summer of 1720, having been seduced by the dream of untold riches, the 'easy money' brigade now sat paralysed, devoid of any strategy, as prices continued to retreat. Instead of selling, they stubbornly held on or even added to their investments whilst the smart money got out. The slide continued from £810 in mid-August to £575 by 9 September; two weeks later the stock value had dropped to £350 and, by the end of the month, the price had fallen to £190, valuing the South Sea Company at just a fifth of its June valuation. A fall of more than 80 per cent in three months wiped out thousands of investors who saw their livelihoods, inheritances and estates disappear. However, those who sold when the price had first started to fall fared better. For example, it was rumoured that one group of investors had banked an estimated £4.5 million by selling their stock as the market turned. Another story from this boom had a very happy ending. Thomas Guy, a Bible seller from London, banked an estimated £250,000 from his investment in the South Sea Company, which he then used to build and finance the now famous Guy's Hospital near London Bridge. Tales of such profits are, however, few and far between and, for the majority, investing in the South Sea Company was a painful experience.

The Roaring Twenties, 1920–29

Following the end of the First World War in 1918, the industrial nations desperately wanted to put this horrific episode behind them and move on towards a happier and more normal way of life. In their eagerness to move their economies forward, the leaders of these nations created an economic environment that encouraged their citizens to follow a capitalist dream to improve their personal lot. Nowhere was this more evident than in the United States. As the war ended a wave of optimism swept the nation. The feel-good factor was supported by rising manufacturing output and economic growth, which in turn saw an increase in personal wealth. An upward spiral of self-feeding positive factors sparked a boom that was to cross almost all asset classes. The United States was finally 'coming of age' and was doing it in style.

Indeed this was a good time to live in the United States. Production and employment were rising and more people were richer than ever before in the nation's history. US capitalism was enjoying a period of tremendous growth. The first investment boom to hit the nation during this period was the great, but short-lived, Florida Real Estate Boom, which occurred in the middle of the decade. Florida had always enjoyed a better climate than New York, Chicago and Washington, particularly in the winter when these cities can suffer the harshest of weather. As incomes increased and improved infrastructure permitted better transportation, middle-class citizens began joining the wealthy in an annual migration south in the winter season. Word soon spread of the potential for economic growth within the 'Sunshine State' and it wasn't long before land promoters were buying up farmland and swampland to be subdivided and sold to eager property speculators. As the prices of both land and any existing properties began to rise, the promise of 'effortless riches' brought even more speculators into the area.

By the autumn of 1925, the congestion of traffic into Florida had become so bad that the railroads were forced to declare an embargo on less essential freight, which included building supplies. The effect on prices was dramatic. Not only were investors scrambling to purchase land to build on, but they were now fighting each other to purchase what few building materials were arriving in the state. The boom was well and truly under way until suddenly Mother Nature decided to intervene. Anyone who has been to Florida on holiday, maybe visiting Disneyland, Seaworld or one of the many other attractions the state now has to offer, will know all about the often violent storms that can hit the area. Only last year whilst on holiday with my family I personally saw the carnage caused by one of these vicious hurricanes. Back in the autumn of 1926, Florida was hit by two such hurricanes, the worst of which killed 400 people and destroyed thousands of houses, leaving approximately 18,000 people in need of help. In a flash, the boom was over. An 'act of God' had given the irrational speculators a severe and painful reality check. Whilst the number of participants in the Florida boom was a great deal smaller than the amount of speculation in the subsequent stock market rally, it still punished many, and it was recorded in the newspapers of the time that nearly every community contained a man who had taken 'quite a beating' in Florida. It's interesting therefore to observe that not only did the real estate collapse fail to dampen the widespread appetite for investing but it actually seemed to encourage it. The mood of this decade was definitely very proactive and positive. Americans felt it was their destiny to move up the ladder and prosper; no wonder it was called the Roaring Twenties.

The surge in the stock market didn't really get under way until the second half of the decade. In fact, 1919–21 actually saw a quite severe bear market as prices retreated 45 per cent from the highs they had recorded following the post-First World War mini-boom driven mainly by the new technology of the era – the automobile. The 1919–21 crash had a severe effect on the US economy with unemployment rising to 12 per cent and both consumer and commodity prices falling. As you would expect, it took a few years for investors to regain their appetite for the market and also for the economy itself to recover. The real stock rally began when the market indices posted new all-time highs in 1925 and, although this coincided with the previously mentioned Florida Real Estate Boom, the stock market move was to last much longer and prices were to rally far higher.

This stock market rally was really a new technology boom, the new technology of the age being the electric utility industry, such as radios, refrigerators, washing machines and toasters, and the automobile industry, where the techniques of mass production pioneered by Henry Ford and FW Taylor brought the ownership of a car into the range of middle-class Americans. An additional boost came from the fact that investors at the time were allowed to purchase stocks and shares posting only 10 per cent of the share price as margin, giving them a massive leverage of 10 to 1. For $100, a speculator could own $1,000 of common stock. Just as in past booms, when investors are offered such a deal in a rising market they grab it with both hands, and this time was no different. Everyone wanted to own these new luxury appliances but none had more appeal than the automobile. It was *the* status symbol – you were nothing without one. It became a self-perpetuating cycle. Americans invested in electric utilities and automobile stocks, the value of these stocks went up and investors then used some of their new profits to buy the luxury 'essential' items produced by the same businesses, pushing their values even higher. Stock prices exploded and investors buoyed with fresh profits, easy margin requirements and a great investment story scrambled to invest even more.

The performance of General Motors' stock price is a great illustration of this process at work. Between the summers of 1925 and 1926, its share price doubled from $50 to $100. In the following 12 months to the summer of 1927, it doubled again to $200, and by the end of the next year, 1928, it had doubled again. Every single year from 1925 up to the Great Crash of 1929, General Motors' share price went up at least 100 per cent. This was an unbelievable performance for such a high-profile company and no wonder investors were falling over themselves to buy stock. From its low of the 1920s, General Motors actually rallied over 2,200 per cent before the October 1929 crash. Another 'new technology' sector that saw tremendous expansion over the decade was radio. In 1920, the United States had only one radio station, yet less than three years later there were over 500 stations broadcasting and, despite the risk of a saturated market, investors piled into the stock of such broadcasters. In one example, the price of RCA (Radio Corporation of America) stock went from a few dollars to over $400 a share. It's easy to see how the broad stock market, driven by the likes of General Motors and RCA, rallied over 600 per cent during this famous bull.

Reviewing the performance of the US stock market we can clearly identify the three stages of this investment boom. Between 1921 and 1925, prices had been slowly moving higher following the bear market at the beginning of the decade. Despite a rally of over 100 per cent, interest in the market was minimal at best, as illustrated by the preference for property over stocks shown at the time during the real estate boom in Florida. Lack of interest despite a price appreciation of 100 per cent is a classic stage one.

Stage two occurred between the summers of 1925 and 1928. During this three-year period share prices doubled again but with far more investor participation. It was becoming easy for 'amateur' investors to make money quickly, a classic condition for this boom to become the topic at every dinner party or social gathering. In addition, a massive improvement in the standard of living for all but the rural poor provided further confirmation that the United States was on its way to everlasting prosperity. The economic model was working; all people had to do was jump on for the ride, and even if they didn't have a great deal of money investors were allowed to leverage aggressively by purchasing stock on a minimal margin.

Most stage three phases of an investment boom tend not to last that long relative to the prior run-up in prices, and the same was true in the Roaring Twenties. The final exponential acceleration in prices lasted barely a year and yet during this period the market doubled again. Speculation reached a fever pitch and, just as with all the investment booms we're examining in this chapter, stage three signalled the beginning of the end. When investors, analysts and market commentators produce crazy, outlandish and illogical justifications for rationalizing why they're still establishing or adding to positions, we should always take this as a warning that the end is nigh. In John Galbraith's excellent account of the 1929 crash he aptly describes this type of period as 'the Twilight of Illusion', and when in such a phase we, as prudent, conservative investors, should get out on the first major drop in prices.

Bad investors are usually quick to enter the market and slow to exit. As we saw with the South Sea Bubble in 1720, when a bull market suddenly turns that's the best time to get out. Don't delay and hold on for a better price; just liquidate your investment and bank the money. Be disciplined. Usually you only get one shot at closing your position at a good level and the crash of 1929 was no different. The carnage not only bankrupted thousands of investors but it also affected millions around the world as it signalled the beginning of the Great Depression.

Such was the pain felt from this crash that many felt it was a lesson learnt and that never again would the 'powers that be' allow the conditions of easy credit and asset inflation to encourage their citizens to speculate their hard-earned money widely with such ease. Unfortunately it was a lesson soon forgotten and it confirms a long-held view that future generations never seem to view a past event in the same way as those who had the bitter first-hand experience.

Japan's asset boom, 1980–89

By the end of the 1980s, Japan's emergence from the ashes of the Second World War to become the fifth-richest nation in the world was the economic success story of the century. The strongest early drivers to its economic recovery lay in the fact that, as a defeated aggressor, Japan, under the terms of its surrender, was not allowed to rebuild the strength of its armed forces. A similar restriction also helped West Germany's post-war growth. When you consider how much money purchasing tanks, jet fighters and warships plus the cost of the personnel required to maintain them can take out of a nation's budget, you can see what a tremendous boost to an economy it would be if the same amount of funds were to be redirected towards building and maintaining domestic industries and infrastructure. This is exactly what happened in Japan. With an emphasis on developing a large and diverse manufacturing base, it exported its way to recovery. Initially the Japanese were just seen as cost-effectively copying existing Western consumables but as their manufacturing expertise increased so they gained a solid reputation for designing and producing their own products. Today, we are all familiar with Japanese brand-name products from televisions and stereo equipment right through to cars and motorcycles. In fact, such is the popularity of Honda, Sony, Yamaha and Suzuki, to name but a few, that today's consumers accept Japanese goods as readily as any produced by home-grown manufacturers.

Japan, its infrastructure, its exports and the performance of its stock market, the Nikkei, became worldwide news, and investors around the globe became eager to participate in the 'Total Quality' philosophy of Japanese business. Two particular asset classes saw tremendous growth in the period between 1945 and 1990, with the majority of the gains occurring in the final 10 years of the period. The first boom was in Japanese property. With a population of approximately 123 million people, Japan was severely overcrowded and, such was the shortage of land available, good property commanded a premium. As they moved away from the rigid 'caste' system in favour of a more Western-style regime, Japanese citizens were able to improve their lives through enterprise and hard work rather than have just the lucky few enjoying their birthright privileges. This new-found entrepreneurial freedom, combined with the country's economic rebound, conspired to make more Japanese affluent than ever before and their first priority appeared to be to upgrade their residential homes. When the stock market rally finally gathered momentum, property values skyrocketed. Between 1986 and 1989, property prices, both residential and commercial, doubled and at their peak, according to Brian Reading's *Japan: The coming collapse* (published by Weidenfeld & Nicolson, 1992), they lost all touch with reality. In 1990, a square yard in the high-class Ginza district reached an astonishing 50 million yen. That meant, if you placed a $1 note on the floor and wanted to purchase the area it covered, it would cost you another $10,000. As an average, Japanese property values at their peak were 10,000 per cent more expensive than values in the United States.

The second boom in the Japanese stock market really picked up pace in the 1980s when the Nikkei 225 Index rallied from 7,000 in 1980 to nearly 40,000 by the end of 1989. During this phenomenal move a number of parallels occurred with past investment trends. Firstly, as with the Dutch Tulip Mania of 1634, financiers invented 'new' and 'sophisticated' financial instruments that encouraged leveraged investing. In another blast from the past, Japanese companies adopted a strategy of borrowing cheap money secured against the ever-rising value of their share price to reinvest in the same asset. Industrial businesses were raising debt not to expand their own operations but to become pure speculators. Japanese corporate executives had created a money merry-go-round. They called this suicidal financial strategy 'zaitech'. The process was something like the now illegal pyramid selling schemes and worked as follows. A company would borrow money against the value of its own rising stock to buy shares. As the stock market moved ever higher, these investments provided the company with new profits, which in turn helped the price of its shares rally again. This rally then allowed the company to go and borrow more money to purchase more shares and so on and so on. In the year to March 1987, the top 10 practitioners of zaitech strategies posted pre-tax profits of $5.3 billion. However, $3.4 billion, over 60 per cent of their overall profits, came from their zaitech operations rather than from their core businesses. Essentially, their profitability was being inflated by the performance of the overall stock market. These figures were also masking the warning signs that something had become seriously wrong with corporate Japan. Since its revival began, Japan had benefited from being an export-led economy. However, this only works if your exports are cheap for other countries to buy. When Japan's currency, the yen, doubled in value against the US dollar between 1985 and 1988, its exports were no longer competitive. The subsequent downturn in sales should have easily been identifiable with a sharp slowdown in corporate performance and a sell-off in the stock market. However, profits were being artificially inflated by zaitech strategies and the economic downturn was masked from all but the very astute. Even the global stock market crash of 1987 couldn't derail the Nikkei. Following a sharp but brief reversal, the Japanese stock market went on to rally another 120 per cent in the two years after October 1987. This resilience in the face of a world crisis further vindicated those still invested in Japan. To these investors it was obvious that the 'Total Quality' approach adopted by Japanese business was a unique and successful model. This blind faith in a new paradigm ended at the beginning of 1990 when the Nikkei 225 Index finally peaked, having rallied over 450 per cent during the previous 10 years.

And yes, you've guessed it, when the end came it was swift and painful, just as it was in every boom we've reviewed so far. Once again, those who cashed in following the first real sell-off in prices were able to bank some healthy profits. However, the vast majority, whom I like to call the 'this time it's different' brigade, adopted the predictable patterns of either holding on to their investments in order to sell next week at a better, higher price or, even worse, increased their positions, rationalizing that the market was now cheap compared to x number of days ago. As you can imagine, all who followed such foolish strategies effectively outstayed their welcome and suffered heavy losses, as the change in this trend was so severe it took less than a year for the Japanese stock market to lose nearly half its value.

The dot.com boom, 1993–2000

The internet first hit the public consciousness in 1993 when stories about the potential of the world wide web began to appear in the financial media. The new information highway really began in earnest the following year when the first web browser became available to the public. Although this investment trend was in its stage one development, a number of astute investors were already beginning to make significant profits in a short period of time, which in turn provided an incentive for others to participate. For instance, investors who bought the stock of Netcom On-Line Communications Services in December 1994 saw their investment grow over 160 per cent by August 1995. Similarly, those who invested in another services provider, UUNET, in the spring of 1995 saw the share price appreciate over 200 per cent in just three months. Another even more spectacular success was the software provider Netscape Communications. On its first day of trading, shares in the company rallied over 165 per cent in a matter of hours and a few months later they had continued their advance by another 130 per cent. Such was the speed and price appreciation of these internet stocks that it led many at the time to question whether this was already a bubble that was about to burst. This is a common mistake people make when they 'finally' discover an investment trend only to realize that it has already significantly risen in value. Nobody likes to miss a good investment opportunity and there is always great satisfaction if you participate in a trend near its beginning. Unfortunately, this usually results in the vast majority mistaking what is actually a stage one/two shift in the trend as a sign that it is nearly over.

If you understand what type of conditions signal stage three, the final stage, of an investment trend, then you would have drawn a very different conclusion to the majority in 1995. Yes, prices were moving higher very quickly and the benchmark index of the tech sector, the Nasdaq, had already doubled in price over the last four years, but there were two key stage three elements missing in 1995. Firstly, there was no widespread public participation and, secondly, there was no media euphoria. In fact, the majority of the general public were still unaware this investment opportunity even existed.

When the madness usually associated with a trend nearing its end finally appeared, it was probably as crazy as anything that has occurred since the Dutch Tulip Mania of the 1630s. One memorable stage three story revolved around the shares of a tiny company called Appian Technology, which traded on the over-the-counter (OTC) market under the ticker symbol 'APPN'. At the same time a private firm, AppNet Systems Inc, decided to go public and registered with the United States regulator. It wanted to trade under the same ticker symbol and therein created the confusion. Although the shares of AppNet Systems were not yet available nor would they be for some time, they were being aggressively touted on internet investors' bulletin boards as the latest dot.com success story. In a massive case of mistaken identity, investors piled into the shares of Appian Technology. All of a sudden, this tiny little company that had been quietly going about its business saw the volume in its shares go from an average of 200 shares traded a day to over 7.3 million in just two days. At the same time its share price rallied 142,757 per cent. No misprint – dot. com investors drove up the price of the wrong company by over one hundred and forty-two thousand, seven hundred and fifty per cent in 48 hours! They bought when in truth they knew nothing about the company they were investing in, not even its true identity. Once again, we can see that the more things change the more they stay the same. At the end of the 20th century in an age that prided itself on fast, accurate information and sophisticated research and advice, investors repeated the mistakes of their predecessors and reverted to a pack of greedy, out-of-control speculators – another example of what John Galbraith called 'the seminal lunacy which has always seized people who are seized in turn with the notion that they can become rich'.

At the peak of the boom, the value of all listed internet companies was in excess of $1.3 trillion and some individual company valuations were unbelievable. Yahoo! was valued at 1,300 times its annual earnings and eBay was valued at 3,300 times its annual earnings. Compare this to the historical market price/earnings average of 15 and these companies were respectively valued at 8,500 per cent and 21,900 per cent above the stock market. A major problem with these valuations was that they had been outrageously high for some considerable time and, if you had based your analysis solely upon such fundamentals, you never even would have participated in them at all and would have missed a phenomenal opportunity to make money. It is in market environments such as this, where investors have lost all touch with reality, that we need to focus our attention on just one piece of data, the price itself. If nothing else makes sense and in reality prices shouldn't be this high, our analysis should concentrate on identifying the point when prices finally appear to respond to the underlying fundamentals. In stage three of an investment cycle, this usually means when prices begin to fall and that's when we need to react quickly and close our positions.

The dot.com boom ended with a sharp rally at the end of 1999 that continued into the new year before the market finally peaked in March 2000 and, just as we have seen throughout this brief study of past booms, when prices go up quickly and then peak they come down at least as fast. This boom was no different and prices fell nearly 40 per cent in just four weeks with the majority of dot.com investors reacting to this fall in just the same way as their predecessors had in 1634, 1720 and 1929. Their disbelief that the good times were over led to a loss-making combination of stubbornness and self-deception and many held on to their positions throughout the subsequent bear market.

To summarize this snapshot review of past investment booms, we have seen:

■ In 1634, over 370 years ago, investors risked their entire livelihoods to purchase a tulip bulb.

- In 1720, over 280 years ago, investors purchased the stock of a company that refused to divulge its true purpose but promised annual returns of 5,000 per cent.
- And in 1999, just six years ago, investors purchased the stock of a company, driving its price up over 140,000 per cent in just two days, without even knowing the company's true identity or the business it conducted.

History confirms:

- Investment booms and bubbles are excellent opportunities to make money.
- In stage one of a boom, prices have gradually begun to rise but not sufficiently for most people to take an interest. It's often hard to obtain detailed research on the potential investment and although it is the most profitable time to establish your position it is also the most difficult phase to identify.
- Stage two is easier to identify because prices are already gaining momentum and sporadic references in the media begin to appear. If you have missed stage one, don't worry, because establishing your position in stage two of the cycle is still a great way to make money. At least half of my profitable investments were established after the trend had entered its second stage.
- Stage three, when prices are accelerating higher and developing an exponential curve, is the beginning of the end. With momentum so strong, this 'new' bull market is now the topic at every social gathering and receives saturation coverage in the media. At this stage, it pays to be on your guard, ready to exit on the first major sign of price weakness. The price direction is always the most important factor.

But history also shows us:

- Stage three phases can continue for long periods of time and on occasions more profit can be achieved by participating in this stage of an investment cycle than in stages one and two combined.
- Patience and discipline make money.
- Fear and greed lose money.

History also confirms my own view that 'greed' is indeed a form of madness, and moving from the 17th and 18th centuries into the modern, sophisticated, well-educated 21st century we can see that nothing has really changed when it comes to how investment booms evolve and how investors continually make the same mistakes. If you're not greedy you can make better, more unemotional and more informed decisions. For a long-term investor, it is imperative to understand how long-term investment trends evolve and how they end.

If you cannot learn from the mistakes made by investors throughout history, you are doomed to repeat them. Ouch!

Long-term investment analysis

The following recommendations form the basis of suggested analytical methods I want you to consider incorporating into an investment strategy. I'm falling short of recommending you religiously follow a rigid system because in truth, whilst the systemized versions of most trend-following strategies are profitable in the long run, they also suffer badly when markets aren't trending. In addition, it's been my experience that, to have the confidence required to follow a system through thick and thin, you need to have developed it yourself. Following somebody else's system is nigh on impossible. As Victor Sperandeo writes in his book *Trader Vic II* (see 'Further reading'), 'to trade a system religiously, you must truly believe in it, and any system I offer here won't mean as much to you as one of your own creation'. Unless you fully understand how a system works in both good times and bad, you'll eventually abandon it. I think the better option is for me to present the primary methods I use to enter and exit trends and for you then to decide whether you want to do the same, change them slightly or research your own. Whilst I'm very happy with using the strategies detailed in this book and they've rewarded me with some fantastic profits over the years, I don't flatter myself in thinking my way is the only way. Obviously, you're more than welcome to adopt my methods – that's why they're included in the book – but the choice of strategy should always be yours. After all, it's your money at risk.

Step 1 – Identify a potential asset class

Identifying stage one of an investment cycle

The type of 'clever', forward-thinking analysis required to pick such a winner is sometimes easier said than done even for a seasoned investor but it is possible to identify the early stages of an investment trend if we know what to look for. Firstly, with stage one moves it's more a case of what you can't find than what you can. It has to be an asset that is not on everyone's radar. It must be unloved by the media and the majority of investors. A simple scan of the financial press and the business sections of the Sunday press may help identify a stage one candidate. Basically, there shouldn't be a great deal of publicity about the asset class. For example, back in the mid-1990s you couldn't find a column inch devoted to investing in property yet prices had already begun to rise. Similarly today, some commodities, such as oil, have only just started receiving press attention yet prices have been rallying for over two years. This early-stage analysis appears a little easier when we consider that there aren't really that many assets/investments to look for in the first place. The following is a list of potential candidates you could be scanning the press for:

■ stock market;
■ stock market sectors (such as healthcare, IT, utilities, pharmaceuticals, etc);
■ commodities;
■ commercial property;
■ residential property;
■ bonds/interest rate products.

If you feel this type of analysis is beyond you, there is an alternative. Find out the asset class or investment opportunities that other successful investors are currently interested in. In Appendix C I have detailed a select group of investment research (newsletter) websites you can access immediately in order to gain such insight. Reviewing the expertise of such renowned market analysts and commentators should guide you towards the right investment opportunities and then you can let the trend-following strategies control the timing of your entries and exits.

Identifying stage two of an investment cycle

If you miss stage one of the cycle, don't despair. Stage two is still a good time to participate and often this stage is a little easier to identify. It is typically the time when more people are becoming aware of the investment opportunity but have still to participate meaningfully. In addition, the media are beginning to devote a little more time and space to the investment story as prices have begun to appreciate noticeably. Again, if you're unsure you can always check out the websites for more information.

Step 2 – Establish your position using charts

Assuming you've identified a potential asset class in which to invest, the next task is to time your entry into the trend successfully, and for that task I recommend you use the study of price charts, which goes under the grand-sounding title of 'technical analysis'. Although it sounds complicated, technical analysis is actually a very basic approach to market price analysis and involves the graphical study of price movements, with charts being the primary tool. Readers who wish to investigate this subject further should review a couple of well-known books, Edwards and Magee's *Technical Analysis of Stock Trends* and John Murphy's *Technical Analysis of the Futures Markets* (see 'Further reading'). Both provide a good grounding in all aspects of the subject.

Before we go any further, let's take a look at the most basic tool of technical analysis, the bar chart. A bar chart is basically a visual representation of a market's price movement where a single vertical bar on the chart displays a market's open, high, low and closing price for a specific period.

As illustrated in Figure 5.1, with a vertical price scale on the far right of the chart and a time period scale running horizontally along the bottom of the chart, each price bar is detailed as follows: the top of each vertical bar (H) represents the highest price the market has traded during the period; the bottom of the bar (L) represents the lowest price it has traded; and the small horizontal dash displayed on the right-hand side of the bar (C) represents the closing price for that period. On some bar charts, you may also find a small horizontal dash displayed on the left-hand side of the bar, which represents the opening price (O). All bar charts display their historical data in the same way, with the oldest data on the far left of the chart through to the most recent market movement detailed on the far right. The charts can represent any period from one minute, where each bar covers just a minute's price information, up to charts where a single bar can represent a whole year. I personally focus upon a weekly bar chart, where each vertical bar represents the opening price, the highest price, the lowest price and the closing price for a single calendar week.

The negatives of technical analysis

Technical analysis is most definitely a 'broad church', for, although it can be described as 'the study of market price action through charts', that is where the simplicity seems to end. Within this broad church, there are numerous different factions that believe that their particular use of charts is the best. There are Gann theorists, Elliott Wavers, MACD users, RSI users, point and figure chartists, bar chartists and candlestick chartists, to name but a few. In fact, there appear to be as many different approaches to studying market price action through charts as there are chartists! It is not my intention to call into question any particular technical analysis approach; suffice to say that over many years of research I have found little of value in most of the indicators and/or guru-type methodologies used by the majority of technical analysts. This may sound strange coming from someone who considers himself a technical analyst, believes in the use of technical analysis and has even been a member of the Society of Technical Analysts but, although I feel this type of market study does have merit, the majority who use it seem to complicate what is essentially

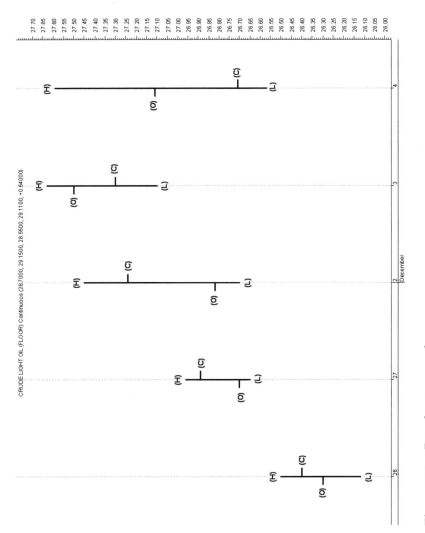

Figure 5.1 Bar chart example

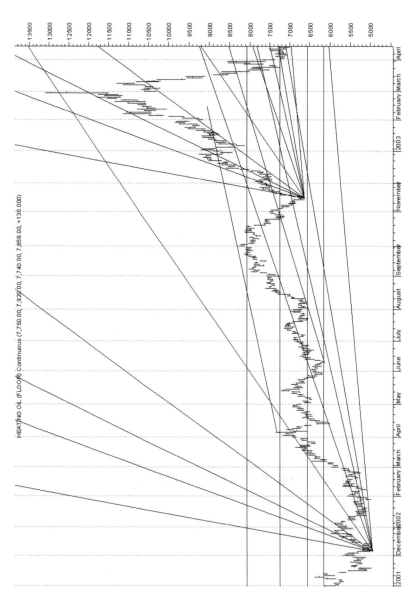

HEATING OIL (FLOOR) Continuous (7,750.00; 7,920.00, 7,740.00, 7,858.00, +130.000)

Figure 5.2 Over-complication of analysis on a chart

a very simple subject. One common misuse is when chartists become preoccupied with predicting which direction the market is heading, announcing price targets or making statements such as 'if the market breaks through 4182 it will go to 5250 but if it breaks 4153 it will go to 3080'. Although the media love this type of analysis, it is generally useless for investing in the markets because the chartist is just spouting levels, which is a futile preoccupation.

Another complication many technical analysts preoccupy themselves with is the drawing of trend lines. The first thing they like to do when they see a chart is grab a pen and ruler and start drawing lines connecting various points in the market together to form a 'trend'. Some chartists draw so many lines it's hard to see the actual market price data, as illustrated by the example in Figure 5.2.

If they can still identify their trend lines through all the mess, these chartists then cling on to them as though they're a safety cable in a high-wire act. Overemphasizing the importance of such trend lines can be costly. In my opinion, you do not need to draw any trend lines on a chart at all. If you look at a chart and you can't immediately identify that the market is in a trend, then it isn't, simple as that. My eight-year-old daughter sometimes sits with me when I'm conducting my weekly analysis and I often pull up a chart on the computer and ask her whether it is trending or ranging (a sideways price action, where the market moves neither up nor down for very long). With no preconceived ideas she simply looks at the screen and states the obvious – what she sees. And, do you know what, she is never wrong – facts are facts.

The positives of technical analysis

Using charts to identify market momentum can be an extremely powerful analytical tool. Used correctly, charts can provide excellent information on the current mood of the market participants, whether they are bullish, bearish or confused. None of this guarantees future success or exactly predicts where a market is heading, but just as a surgeon uses an ECG to determine a patient's condition so can a technical analyst use charts to get a handle on the market's recent and current condition. This is because the market price as represented on a chart is the sum total of all the rumours, gossip, fundamental information and sentiment currently in circulation at the time. Regardless of what people say or have an opinion about, it's what they do that counts, and when they invest or liquidate their cash it affects the price. If investors are bullish they will enter the market and it will rally; if they are bearish they will liquidate and the market will fall.

> I agree with the metaphysics of technical analysis that the fundamentals are discounted. You don't get any profits from fundamental analysis; you get profit from buying and selling. So why stick with the appearance when you can go right to the reality of price and analyze it better.
>
> Legendary multimillionaire futures trader Richard Dennis

Technically speaking, I believe in keeping your analysis as simple and straightforward as possible and, although over the years I've experimented with numerous different methods including complicated computer programs and abstract algorithms, through both historical testing and real-time investing I've whittled my approach down to just a few technical strategies. In addition to their simplicity, these strategies have also stood the test of time with variations of each approach applied successfully and profitably by many highly respected investors over the last 40 years.

Recommended investment strategies

> ... economics is not an exact science; it consists merely of Laws of Probability. The most prudent investor, therefore, is one who pursues only a general course of action which is 'normally' right and who avoids acts and policies which are 'normally' wrong.
>
> LLB Angas

Trend following by definition is a reactive method of operation because first we need to identify there is a trend before we can follow it. Market prices have to make the first move and, if you decide to become a trend follower, you must accept that you will never establish a position whilst prices are at their lowest. I've already covered the psychological pressures of following such an approach so let's now look at some of the actual strategies I use in my own long-term investment analysis. I recommend you consider incorporating them or variations of them into your own analysis but I also encourage you to research other methods as well, and in the 'Further reading' section towards the end of this book I have detailed a number of titles you should consider purchasing to enhance your knowledge of this subject further.

My personal investment analysis is very simple in that I prefer to concentrate primarily upon the weekly movements in price as detailed on a bar chart (see Appendix C for a list of suggested charting websites and software providers). I've spent over 20 years participating in the markets and during this time experimented with many forms of both fundamental and technical analysis. The strategies I use today are the result of both this personal experience and historical research. They work and they also suit my style of long-term investing.

Use weekly data

My preference for using weekly data, and more importantly the closing price on the last trading day of the week, is that it generally removes the effect short-term speculators have on the market and provides a fair representation of the positions held by medium- to long-term investors, for it's they who ultimately participate in the major market trends. Shorter-term speculators are responsible for a tremendous amount of irregular price movements known as 'noise'. These price fluctuations often appear random in nature and are extremely unpredictable and also meaningless to long-term market direction, so it is in my interest to mitigate the effect they have on my long-term analysis. Focusing upon the final closing price of the week normally removes a large percentage of these participants, as they tend to be uncomfortable with having any market exposure over a weekend and usually close all their outstanding positions by the closing bell on the final trading day of the week. This means the actual movement of the market from last week's final closing price to this week's final closing price will generally represent the net effect of the involvement of medium- to long-term investors. For example, if this week's closing price is higher than last week's closing price, it indicates that buyers have been willing to pay higher prices to establish their positions and/or that those who had previously sold the market were prepared to pay higher prices to close their positions. This is a bullish market condition. Conversely, if this week's closing price is lower than last week's, it indicates that sellers have been willing to establish short positions at lower prices and/or that those who had previously bought the market were prepared to sell at lower prices to close their positions. This is a bearish market condition. In isolation you can't read too much into a single week's performance but it is a useful data point for input into longer-term market analysis.

When to invest

Richard Donchian

Whilst I'd love to claim the credit for these strategies, I have to acknowledge the 'father of trend following', Richard Donchian, as the inspiration behind them. As well as being a pioneer of technical trend-following strategies, Donchian is also famous for being the founder of the managed money industry, having started his first managed fund way back in 1949.

Born in Hartford, Connecticut in 1905, he graduated with a BA in economics from Yale in 1928. Despite initially losing a considerable amount of money in the crash of 1929, he continued to study the markets and, in 1930, began using price chart-based strategies over and above fundamental information. Spurred on by an early investment success in the automobile sector, Donchian began writing a technical market letter for Hemphill, Noyes & Co in 1933. His financial career was suspended during the Second World War, when he served as a statistical control officer for the United States Air Force. He returned to Wall Street after the war, joining Shearson Hamill & Co. In 1960, he moved to Hayden, Stone where he was employed as a vice-president and as director of commodity research. It was during this period of his career that his real pioneering technical work was conducted and his weekly newsletter, 'Trend timing comments', became a must-read for all technically-minded traders and investors.

By the mid-1970s, Donchian was managing a considerable amount of client money, and his income from both advisory fees and profits from investing his own money was estimated to be over $2 million a year – not an insignificant amount for the time. Two of the technical systems Donchian used at this time also form the basis for my own analysis and, whilst I have adjusted both the time-frames and certain other aspects of each approach, the core logic behind their application and success remains the same.

Follow momentum – use a moving average

The first Donchian-based system utilized the moving average (MA). A moving average is one of the most basic yet effective trend-following technical analysis tools available to the investor. Essentially, all a moving average does is smooth out the price fluctuations of a market by averaging the closing prices for a certain period of time, providing a clearer visual picture of the major trends over the same period. Donchian's original system was applied to the commodity and futures markets and stated that, whenever the 5-day MA had a higher figure than the 20-day MA, the market should be bought and, whenever the 5-day MA had a lower figure than the 20-day MA, the market should be sold. His system guaranteed that, if a market trend occurred in either direction, then Donchian and his clients would establish their positions and benefit from any future continuation of that trend.

Donchian's original use of moving averages was far shorter-term than I feel comfortable with as a long-term investor and so, to monitor a longer-term time-frame, I use a single moving average covering an extended period. In the stock market, many technicians follow a 200-day moving average, often recommending shares should be purchased if the current price is above the 200-day moving average and then liquidated when the current price falls below it. It is a widely touted indicator and, as such, deserves to be considered, because the greater the number of market participants who use it the greater its influence can often be. Because my analysis is conducted weekly and I only use weekly charts, I adapted the 200-day MA into a 40-week MA (200 days divided by 5 days a week = 40 weeks). In addition, I'm not interested just in whether prices are above or below the moving average but am also concerned with the momentum of the moving average itself.

For example, a 40-week MA would indicate the average weekly closing price of the last 40 weeks and, if it is increasing in value, this indicates to me that the market is gaining long-term upward (bullish) momentum. Conversely, if the 40-week MA begins to fall in value, this indicates long-term downward (bearish) momentum. Because manually recording the necessary amount of weekly data to construct a long-term weekly moving average is going to take you a long while, I would encourage you to use one of the many free-access charting websites available (contact information in Appendix C) to construct a moving average and conduct your analysis. Although I do not encourage you to calculate a moving average manually because it's too time consuming, let's quickly review the process so you understand exactly how one is constructed. To calculate a 40-week MA manually, you need the weekly closing prices (this is the closing price of the market on the last trading day of the week, typically a Friday except for the odd bank holiday) for the most recent 40 weeks. To get a moving average figure, you simply add up those 40 weekly closing prices to get a cumulative figure and then divide by 40. This final figure represents the current 40-week MA (the average weekly closing price for the last 40 weeks). In subsequent weeks, to get the current 40-week MA figure simply repeat the process by adding up the most recent 40 weeks' closing prices and divide by 40. This process is repeated at the end of every trading week.

Method 1

Using a 40-week moving average, the first method I offer for your consideration is:

Only invest or stay invested in a market where the current weekly closing price is above the current 40-week MA and the trend of that 40-week MA is upwards.

It might also be helpful to look at this method in a different way:

You should *never* invest or stay invested in a market where the current weekly closing price is below the current 40-week MA.

And:

> You should *never* invest or stay invested in a market where the trend of the 40-week MA is down.

The example in Figure 5.3 illustrates a classic 40-week MA entry signal. Weekly prices have begun to rally and they are above a rising 40-week MA.

The primary purpose of this method is to help you get in and/or help you stay in a trend when its momentum is up. The moving average itself can often be too slow and insensitive to act as a consistent form of analysis for closing a position but it is very helpful in providing you with the discipline to run profits, and the ability to run your profits is the key to successful trend following. Running your profits means resisting the temptation to close your investment position just because its profits have already exceeded your expectations. Without a disciplined approach, it's psychologically very hard to contain the obvious excitement of seeing your money growing day by day and not attempt to second-guess where or when the market is going to peak. This will usually result in you closing your position too soon. When I was working in the City I often used to hear the phrase, 'You'll never go broke taking a quick profit.' This may be true but I also believe you'll never get rich taking a quick profit.

Such is the mental torment at the possibility of allowing large chunks of unrealized profit to slip through their fingers that some investors follow a strategy of setting price targets to liquidate their investments. They rationalize through various methods of analysis that, if an investment is at a certain level and then trebles in value, they will close their position, bank the profit and move on to another opportunity. Whilst following this type of strategy does indeed guarantee they will bank some profits, it could also force them to close a great investment position too early. To give you an example, many years ago I had a client who made the following mistake. Shrewdly, he had purchased shares in a US computer software company at an average of around $8 per share. At this point in his career, he used price targets to liquidate all his positions, and when the shares hit his target level of $16 he promptly closed his position, banking a very healthy 100 per cent profit on the investment. Unfortunately for him, though, this was just the beginning

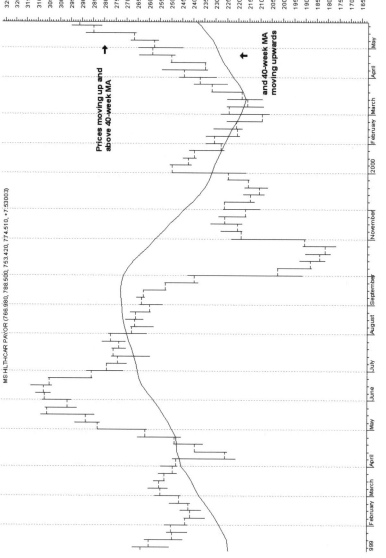

Figure 5.3 Weekly bar chart with rising 40-week moving average

of a tremendous upward move that saw the shares reach $60 before finally peaking. He watched this trend continue in disbelief – a further 275 per cent gain from where he had closed his position. If he had been a trend follower using my strategies, I calculated he would have achieved an additional profit of about $6 million – a nice return for no extra work!

Whilst it's true that trends such as this don't occur very often, when they do you should have a strategy that helps you capture as much of the move as realistically possible. That's the purpose of the 40-week moving average and that's why I use it. This strategy doesn't work every time but, when it does, the profits are far greater than anything the vast majority of investors could achieve from participating in the same trend.

Weekly Rule – upside breakouts

The second strategy I use is another developed by Richard Donchian and focuses upon a simple chart pattern, the price channel breakout. A large number of successful trend followers use channel breakouts as either primary or secondary indicators. In fact, if we think about it logically, no market can rally very far without generating a significant 'breakout' signal. Chart breakouts guarantee you will never miss participating in a major bull trend in the markets you are monitoring. Labelled by Donchian as the 'Weekly Rule', his original system generated a buy signal whenever the market price moved above the highest high of the last four weeks. This position was then held until the price moved below the lowest low of the last four weeks, when the position was reversed. Donchian's system ensured you always held a position in the market and that you were guaranteed to participate in every trend both up and down. This approach has been reviewed with critical acclaim by many eminent market researchers and technicians for both its simplicity and profitability.

Although Donchian's Weekly Rule system was undoubtedly successful, it would occasionally fall foul of the curse of any trend-following-based approach, namely the non-trending market. Markets can often spend a large percentage of their time without any sustained trends, and these non-trending periods often create numerous false signals known in market terminology as 'whipsaws'. To avoid some of these

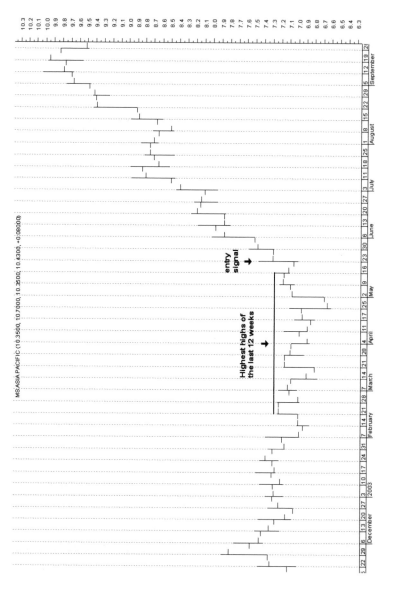

Figure 5.4 Weekly bar chart with 12-week upside breakout signal

whipsaw signals, technical analysts created a number of variations to the Weekly Rule, which involved extending the time-frame of the price channel and/or stipulations that the market must actually close beyond the highest high or lowest low before a signal was generated. Following historical research and years of real-time investing, my variation of this indicator also involves extending the time-frame and additionally requires the market to post a weekly close above the highest high.

Method 2

> Establish a position when the current week's closing price is the highest price of the last 12 weeks.

In market terminology this is known as an 'upside breakout'. The beauty of using a breakout approach if you are a trend follower is that it's guaranteed to get you in every long-term trend. It has to, because for any market to move meaningfully upwards it will, at some point, have to break up to new higher levels and generate a signal as illustrated in the example in Figure 5.4. The reason I use a 12-week breakout is that by covering approximately a three-month period of prices it reduces the number of false signals generated by random price movements. Nothing can protect you from the odd false move, but a 12-week parameter is insensitive enough to miss most of the market noise whilst still sensitive enough to get in a trend near the beginning. Utilizing an upside breakout strategy epitomizes the golden rule of trend following – buy strength.

Combining methods 1 and 2

Another tactic you can consider is to combine both the moving average and channel breakout methods, only establishing a position when the market satisfies both criteria. The combined rules look like this:

Entry: Only establish an investment position when the current weekly close is the highest price of the last 12 weeks and it is above the current 40-week MA and the trend of that 40-week MA is upwards.

Position running: Stay invested as long as the current weekly close is above the current 40-week MA and the trend of that 40-week MA is upwards.

In Figure 5.5, we can see the two methods working together on the same chart. Combining two solid long-term trend-following rules in this way is a tactic used by some of the most successful technically based fund managers and investors in the world. Their respective time-frames may be different but the strategy of only acting on breakouts supported by a positive moving average signal has stood the test of time.

Troubleshooting

Let's assume you've just read this book and on your first weekly analysis you see the chart in Figure 5.6.

The natural reaction is to wish you'd seen this chart and invested five months ago when the market first broke up at level A. Feeling disappointed at already missing out on such a great trend most investors will now find it psychologically impossible to establish a position a full 40 per cent higher at level B. Whenever such a situation as this occurs, I ignore the past price action and simply apply my analysis to the current weekly chart. When the next entry signal is generated, I establish a position. Although, just like everyone else, I would have preferred to have invested in this market earlier, at far better levels, I'm still happy to invest now. The correct mantra for successful trend following is 'BUY HIGH to SELL HIGHER'. Don't beat yourself up if a trend is already established when you first begin conducting your analysis. Just establish a position whenever the next entry signal is generated because in the long run this will work in your favour.

The same tactics also apply to a market where you have already participated in a trend and closed your position, only to see the market rally again to new highs, generating a new entry signal. Although the trend itself may appear mature, I always act upon such a signal. It could be that the trend has further to run and the recent sell-off was nothing more than a pause. It is not uncommon for some of the most powerful trends to exhibit such behaviour and in the past I've participated in a number of powerful trends where numerous entry and exit signals have been generated. As you will see from an example included later in the book, when numerous signals are generated you must remain disciplined and follow your strategies because nobody, professional or amateur, fund manager or analyst, producer or consumer, actually knows when a trend will begin or end. Even those with illegal inside information get it wrong. At best, any form of market analysis is calculated guesswork, and preoccupying your thoughts with how mature the trend may appear or deliberating over whether you should accept or decline the next entry signal can be an expensive waste of your time and money.

Perhaps the hardest thing for an investor to do psychologically is enter a market that is making record all-time highs. It's tough because relatively speaking the investment will seem expensive. For example, if the price of a stock or commodity has never in its entire history traded higher than $40 and historically averaged between $8 and $25, would you act upon a signal to invest at $42? The vast majority of the investment community wouldn't because they always compare today's price to the historically high levels where the market last peaked and such a comparison would make a purchase level of $42 seem both expensive and risky. People tend to visualize the future as they see the present, good or bad. However, all-time highs can be a strategically important event, a paradigm shift. Firstly, markets whose prices break up to new all-time highs are often indicating that a fundamental change has occurred and whatever has happened in the past shouldn't apply any more. Secondly, because this is the first time the price has reached this level, there will be no selling pressure from speculators covering losing positions – in fact, quite the opposite, because as the market moves higher those who sold short (a process where speculators sell now, hoping to buy back the position at a profit in the future at a lower level) because they thought the price was already too high will eventually have to cover their losing positions, adding further buying impetus. The truth is, whenever a market breaks upwards into virgin territory (it has never traded there before), it is the most bullish situation in which to invest or remain invested. So never hold back. If your analysis generates an entry signal with prices at their all-time highs, it may feel uncomfortable but, in actual fact, it can be the best time to invest.

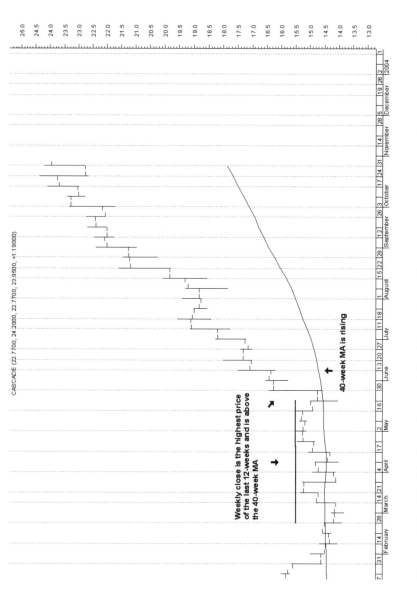

Figure 5.5 Weekly bar chart with rising 40-week moving average and 12-week upside breakout signal combined

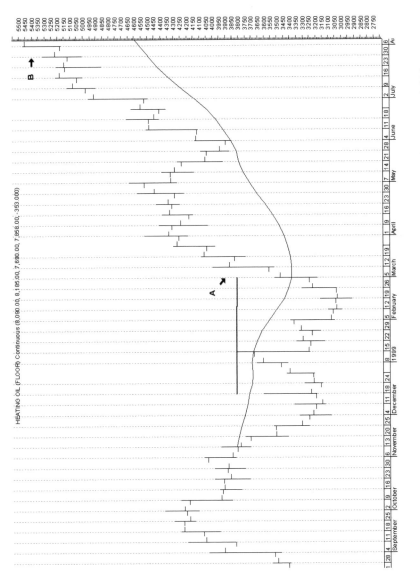

Figure 5.6 Weekly bar chart with mature trend (B) from a missed buy signal (A)

Successful trend following is about identifying and then following the momentum of a market. Focus on buying price strength and selling price weakness: buying high to sell even higher.

To recap the entry tactics: 1) use stage analysis and your own or suggested research to identify a potential investment trend; and 2) use technical analysis (chart-based) momentum strategies to time your entries.

And remember, the price action of an investment as detailed on a bar chart should always have the final say in whether or not you participate. Follow upward price momentum.

When to liquidate

Exit analysis needs to be different

To be honest, getting in is the easy part. Now we need to look at the most challenging aspect of investing – when to liquidate your position: when to get out. It has been my experience that it pays to use additional strategies for identifying when to close our investment positions than we used to establish them. This is because long-term trend-following approaches are usually too slow in reacting to a change in trend from up to down. The characteristics of a bull market that make it easy for long-term trend-following strategies to participate can also work against you if you only employ the same strategies to liquidate as well. Bull markets, by definition, involve an increase in price and valuations, which in turn creates wealth for those invested. As investors tend to accumulate their positions over long periods of time and good news on the economy or company sales or supply and demand is drip-fed into the market, a bull market trend will usually take a long time to unfold. This type of market price movement allows plenty of time for even the slowest trend-following method to generate an entry signal. However, when a bull market ends, the downward shift in momentum is typically faster owing to the fact that a reversal in prices equals a reversal in the fortunes of investors. Bad news is normally the catalyst for the liquidation of positions and this tends to hit the market with far more force than the good news ever did. It can set off a chain reaction. As investors see their unrealized profits disappear they begin selling to close their own positions for fear of further profit erosion, which then sends prices down further, forcing even more investors to liquidate. That's why the behaviour of a market at these turning points is very different from that in the rest of the trend. The sharp and often vicious retracement in prices that characterizes the end of a boom is usually too quick for most long-term trend-following strategies to identify satisfactorily and that is the reason why I personally include additional methods of analysis to close my positions.

As I've mentioned before, you shouldn't ever expect to close your investment at the top of a trend. If you do, then accept you got lucky. But by the same token, neither do you want to give back large chunks of any unrealized profits before receiving an exit signal. In an ideal world, we want a strategy insensitive enough to keep you in a trend but sensitive enough to get you out when that trend finally ends. Developing exit strategies is definitely more of an art than a science but there are one or two things I incorporate into my analysis that can put the odds more in my favour and I recommend you consider using them as well.

Use 'stage analysis'

When implementing an exit strategy, the first priority, just as with identifying a potential investment entry, is to establish at what stage of an investment trend the market actually is. If we can identify that a market has entered its euphoric stage three phase when everyman and his dog wants to participate and the media are full of headlines and 'expert' analysis, then we should take this as a warning that the trend is maturing and could be vulnerable. As we have reviewed earlier in the book, stage three is the final phase of an investment trend but it doesn't necessarily mean the end is coming any time soon. Markets can stay in a stage three phase for a long while so it would be imprudent to close a position just because prices are rising and your doctor or dustman is also participating in the same markets. However, if you identify such a market condition you need to remain alert and ready to act on the first sign of a change in momentum. When that happens you must close your position at the first opportunity. Don't hang in there for a higher price. If you remember our review of past investment booms you will recall that when the end comes it is usually swift and severe. Do not hesitate or try to be clever at this stage – *just get out*!

Change in momentum

One clear warning that will alert you that a bull market is nearing the end is when prices begin to rally exponentially compared to the trend's prior momentum. Such an exponential price movement is unsustainable in the long run and, when prices rally in such a fashion, they often quickly reverse direction with a violent move down. If you identify such a reversal, this is a signal to close your position.

Method 3

If a market rallies exponentially, liquidate following the first big reaction in price.

In Figure 5.7, the exit signal (A) is the first major reaction following an exponential rally in prices.

Psychologically, closing your position following such a price movement can be a tough decision because prices often fall quickly and you'll be well aware of the amount of unrealized profit you have already lost by not selling at the top of the market. Closing the position will feel wrong because you would have preferred to have exited earlier at a higher level and bank more profits. My recommendation in such an environment is to forget about what could have or should have been; just accept the profits you've still got and close the position.

Method 4

Another indication that an investment trend could be over is a sharp reaction against the prevailing trend without any prior warning.

If a market unexpectedly posts a large, sharp reaction against the prevailing trend, liquidate the position.

In Figure 5.8, a strong consistent trend suddenly collapses, posting a violent reaction in prices.

When you experience such a price movement, the best tactic is, once again, to close your position. Typically, a market will just stop dead in its tracks and reverse direction without any prior warning

– no stage three euphoria or recent exponential price movement. Sometimes, this reaction is in response to a widely publicized external event and sometimes it isn't – the market just falls. However, such a price reaction is a visual clue that something in the market could have fundamentally changed. In strong consistent trends, reactions like this rarely occur and so the risk reward favours closing your position. If the trend has ended, the retracement could be swift and unforgiving. Your reactions need to be exactly the same – swift and unforgiving. Do not get 'married' to your investment. It is not a relationship that should contain 'for better or worse', 'for richer or poorer' or 'till death do us part' loyalties. You need to be fickle and, as soon as the market makes you feel uncomfortable, dump your investment and move on to the next opportunity.

On some occasions this sharp counter-trend reaction may be a false move known in market terminology as a 'shake-out'. If this is the case and the market immediately reverses and continues back upwards again, you can always reapply the 40-week moving average and/or the 12-week breakout entry strategies to re-establish your position. However, it's just as common to see a sharp reaction like this spell the end of a trend.

The bottom line is – if a market trend that has previously been very kind and profitable to you turns around and bites you, get out and get out fast, because the likelihood is the game has changed.

Always safety first.

The preservation of your investment capital and any unrealized profit has to be your main concern. Establishing an investment position isn't a particularly stressful experience but closing one often can be. When prices fall we all experience a number of emotions from shock and disbelief to anger and frustration. For undisciplined investors this can often induce a form of mental paralysis and their usual reaction is to stare trance-like at their charts, the market price quotes on their computer screens or the financial television channels. At this point, some investors incorrectly adhere to the 'When in doubt, do nothing' mantra. However, this type of wisdom only applies to establishing an investment. If you already hold a position and the market turns nasty and you're still not quite sure what the correct tactic should be, you've always got to think, 'When in doubt, get out!' You may feel disappointed at giving back some unrealized profits but think how

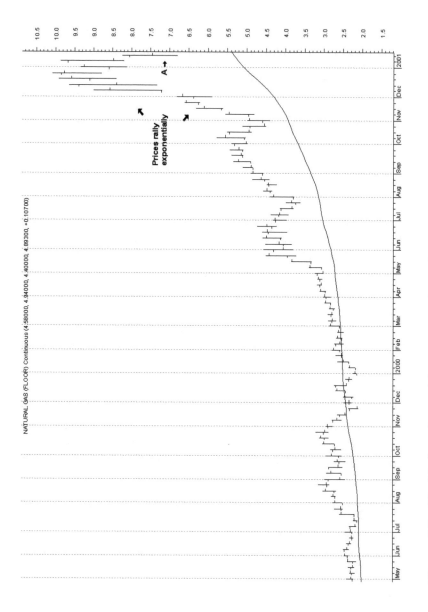

NATURAL GAS (FLOOR) Continuous (4.58000, 4.94000, 4.40000, 4.89300, +0.107000)

Prices rally
exponentially

A

Figure 5.7 Weekly bar chart with exponential trend

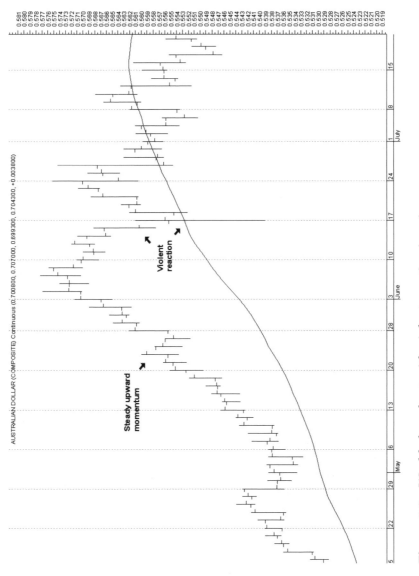

Figure 5.8 Weekly bar chart with violent reaction in price

you'll feel if you continue to hold the position and the market drops even further.

To recap the exit tactics: 1) use stage analysis to identify when the trend has entered its stage three ending phase; and 2) use technical analysis (chart-based) momentum strategies to time your exits.

And remember, the price action of an investment as detailed on a bar chart should always have the final say in whether or not you continue to participate in a trend. Regardless of whether a trend appears to have entered a stage three phase or not, if the downward price momentum is strong enough it carries greater significance than any other input and you should liquidate your position.

Think, always safety first.

Conducting your analysis

Using the strategies detailed in this book shouldn't take more than an hour a week to complete, and I think it's very important to maintain a regular routine for conducting this analysis. Set aside a quiet period of time, when there will be no distractions and you can focus entirely on the job at hand. I prefer to operate when the markets are closed and typically conduct my chart analysis at the weekend, when I can easily review the past week's price action. Then, when the markets reopen at the beginning of the following week, I'm ready to issue my broker with any new orders.

Another factor I believe is important to the quality of your market analysis is where you operate. I recommend you set aside a dedicated area of your home where you can shut yourself away from distractions. Sitting at the kitchen table whilst your kids or spouse chat, fight, watch TV or eat dinner is not going to help you concentrate. I use a study at home but you don't need anything as grand. Providing you can connect your PC to the internet (see Appendix C for a list of suggested free-access charting websites), you can base yourself anywhere; just make sure it's free from distraction. Remember, the quality of the time you spend reviewing your investments is more important than the quantity of time you devote, and even the most innocuous interruption could result in you missing a signal.

Another often overlooked but important aspect of long-term investing is record-keeping. I keep a record of all my investments in a diary specifically purchased for the purpose. It's paramount that you record every position you open and close, including the time you telephoned your broker, the name of the individual to whom you gave your instructions and the prices at which you either bought or sold. Then, when the broker sends its statements you can reconcile its records with yours. Mistakes don't happen very often but they do occur now and again and, if you don't correct them, it could cost you money.

To recap: 1) regularly conduct your analysis in a quiet location, free from distraction; and 2) keep your records up to date and reconciled with your broker's statements.

Over the next few years, I believe the commodity markets will be the best opportunity for you to make some serious money and, if you're disciplined, participating only when your analysis generates an entry signal, you will have an excellent chance of profiting handsomely.

In addition, as the trend-following strategies recommended in this book will focus you on investing in assets that have begun to appreciate in value and liquidating assets that have begun to fall in value, they can have numerous other applications as well. The prerequisite for their application is whether the value of the asset in question can be monitored on a regular and impartial basis. For instance, any major stock market index such as the Dow Jones Industrial, Nasdaq Composite or FTSE 100 would be OK, as would individual stocks, mutual funds or any other publicly quoted investment vehicles. In fact, I used variations of these strategies to good effect when buying residential property through monitoring the monthly produced Halifax House Price Index, which provided an excellent entry signal on UK residential property in 1994 after house values had rallied from their 1992 low. After that, the average UK house price as measured by the price index and confirmed by my own experience went on to more than double in value over the next nine years.

In summary, I buy what's going up. If it keeps going up, I hold on to the position, and when it finally starts to go down I sell and get out. It's a very simple philosophy but it's made me a lot of money.

Trends persist.

Richard Donchian

A personal example

To further your understanding of how my strategies work, I thought it would be useful to provide a blow-by-blow account of one of my past investments. The entire trend itself lasted over five years and as you'll see my methods coped well, but as is the way with investing it wasn't all plain sailing. I hope the following gives you a feel for how trend following works and a little taster of what you may have to cope with yourself. The investment trend I want to review occurred between 1995 and 2000 and the market I participated in was the Standard & Poor's 500 Composite Index (S&P 500).

The S&P 500 is an index comprising the 500 largest capitalized companies listed on the main US stock exchanges. Of the 500 constituents, 424 stocks are listed on the New York Stock Exchange (NYSE), 74 on the National Association of Securities Dealers Automated Quotation System (Nasdaq) and 2 on the American Stock Exchange (AMEX). The S&P 500 is calculated using the 'market value-weighted method'. This is where a company worth $6 billion is given twice the weighting of a company worth $3 billion. It is the best way of creating a market index, as it allows investors to capture total economic activity and the changes in valuation of the United States' top companies. The logic is that, by giving the larger capitalized companies a higher weighting, the method is reflecting the fact that the largest companies generally have the largest revenues and profits.

Figure 5.9 is a weekly bar chart covering the entire trend from the beginning to the end of my participation but, before I recount the individual entries and exits, I want to provide you with a brief overview of the sentiment towards the United States stock market leading up to the end of 1994. Following the October 1987 crash, the market had spent the next couple of years regaining lost ground and, as it entered the 1990s, the S&P 500 was once again posting new all-time highs. This momentum was rudely interrupted in October 1990 with another severe sell-off, although the market once again recovered quickly to post new highs by the spring of 1991. The next three years up until the spring of 1994 saw the market post some consistent if not exactly spectacular returns. Despite this steady rise the general mood was fairly apathetic towards stocks and, when the S&P 500 dropped over 6 per cent in the spring of 1994 wiping out nearly all the previous

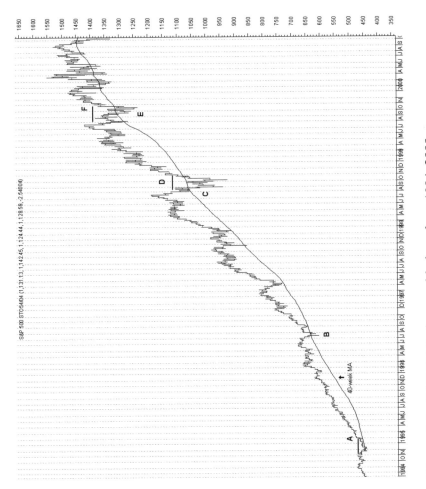

Figure 5.9 S&P 500 Index weekly bar chart 1994–2000

12 months' gains, the sentiment actually became bearish. Professionals and amateurs alike publicly stated that they felt this market had already gone too far and, to sum up the mood at the time, one of the best-selling business books was titled *Bankruptcy 1995*. As the market spent the rest of 1994 in a lifeless sideways crawl, the mood became even more bearish. Everybody seemed to feel the stock market was ready for a major fall. Therefore, you can imagine the shock and disbelief that greeted a New Year's rally at the beginning of 1995. Personally, I had no strong view on the stock market, although owing to the bearish sentiment I did consider the possibility of a small rally. Anyhow, it didn't really matter as I always leave the decision-making process to my strategies, and it wasn't long before the markets had generated an entry signal (A), as shown in Figure 5.10.

In Figure 5.10, you can clearly see the 40-week moving average line moving in an upward direction, with the weekly market close (A) recorded on 3 February 1995 above the moving average line and also the highest price of the last 12 weeks. In addition, this rally in prices was met with even more bearish market comment and analysis. This is a classic stage one scenario – prices are moving significantly higher and nobody believes the move. This, coupled with the chart confirmation, was my entry signal and I established a position at the beginning of the following week at 479.20.

The next 16 months went like a dream as the market rallied over 40 per cent in virtually one straight line until summer 1996.

Figure 5.11 illustrates a classic market 'shake-out'. From the high recorded nine weeks prior to the intra-week low (B), the market pulled back less than 6 per cent to close on 19 July 1996 just above the 40-week MA. Although the reason for this retracement is now lost to me, I can tell you from reading the records I kept at the time that this was no stage three price action. In fact, my analysis concluded that, despite a strong performance over the last year or so, the stock market was still in a stage one phase characterized by a complete apathy towards the recent gains. Therefore, with a still rising 40-week MA, my tactics were to sell if the market closed below the intra-week low of 605.88 (B). Despite a similar sell-off the following week, this level was never broken and the market soon resumed its upward march much to the continued disbelief of the masses.

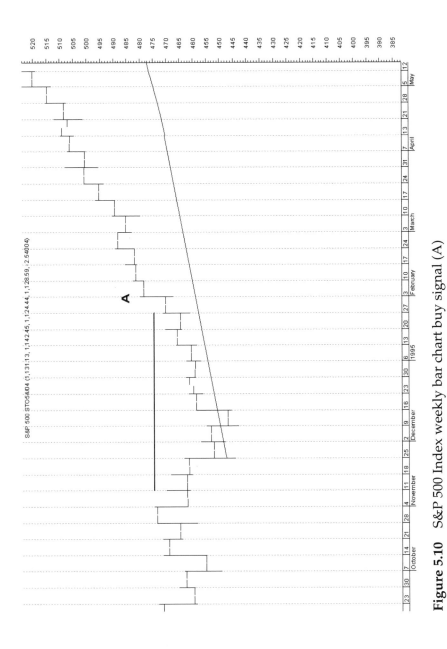

Figure 5.10 S&P 500 Index weekly bar chart buy signal (A)

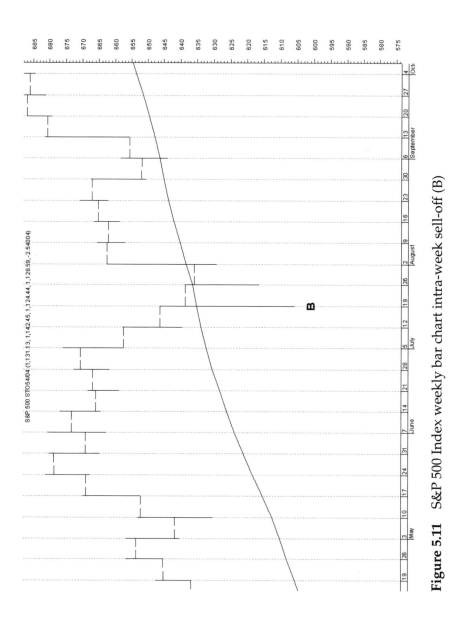

Figure 5.11 S&P 500 Index weekly bar chart intra-week sell-off (B)

Fast-forward two years and, yes, I was still invested. The market had now rallied 150 per cent since I first invested back in February 1995 and as you can imagine following such a fantastic performance everybody was now bullish on the stock market.

Reviewing the analysis I recorded at the time, I appeared to be unsure whether the market was in a stage two or a stage three phase. Sentiment had become very bullish, yet the rally in prices during the first six months of 1998 had not been exactly exponential. Granted the rally was a strong one, but it was virtually identical to the rally seen during the early months of 1997. As I've said before, always let the price charts guide you, and that's what I did in the autumn of 1998. As illustrated in Figure 5.12, following a brief rally to new highs in July the market quickly reversed and then drifted lower for a few weeks before significantly closing below the 40-week MA on the week ending 28 August (C). From a stage analysis perspective I was confused and so I took my cue from the charts and acknowledged the close below the moving average as a signal to liquidate my investment, which I did at the beginning of the following week. My banked profit on this investment after all brokerage costs was over 100 per cent. Had I concluded the market was in a stage three phase, that would have been the end of my involvement. However, as you know, I was undecided at the time and so, when the market promptly reversed direction and rallied again above the still rising 40-week MA and posted a 12-week highest close (D) on the week ending 6 November, I re-established my position, re-entering the market at 1143.50. With the benefit of hindsight the price action that signalled my initial exit from the market was nothing more than a 'shake-out'. Such is life; we can't be correct all the time.

The next action occurred 12 months later and it was to spell the end of my involvement in the stock market. Following the 1998 shake-out, I was watching the media coverage of the stock market more closely than ever. The dot.com boom was well under way and there were a number of Sunday supplement articles appearing featuring 'average' people who had left their mundane jobs to speculate full time in the stock market. The confirmation that this trend was now in stage three of its cycle was the publicity surrounding the imminent publication of a new investment book bearing the title *Dow 36,000*. Considering at the time that the level of the Dow Jones Industrial Average was around 10,500, you could see why I felt the stock market had entered its final

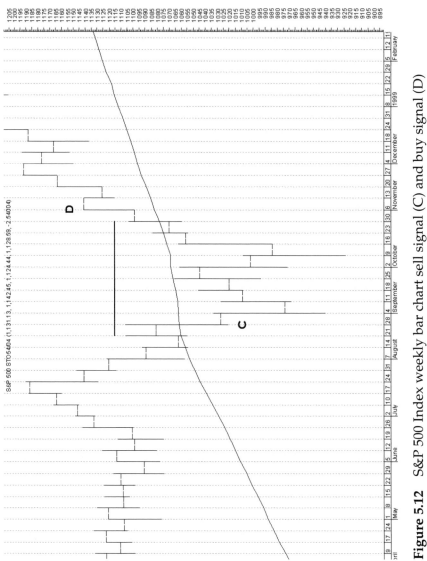

Figure 5.12 S&P 500 Index weekly bar chart sell signal (C) and buy signal (D)

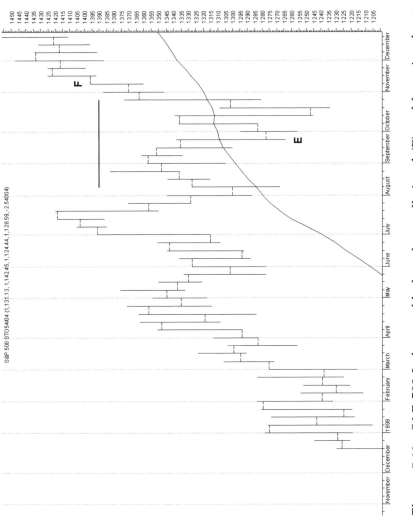
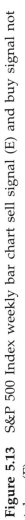

Figure 5.13 S&P 500 Index weekly bar chart sell signal (E) and buy signal not taken (F)

stage. Stage three is the final phase of a trend but it doesn't necessarily mean the end is coming any time soon. Once again the best tactic in these situations is to rely upon chart price action to determine when to close our positions.

For me, this occurred on the week ending 24 September 1999 when the market posted a significant weekly close below the 40-week moving average (E), as shown in Figure 5.13. I closed my position at the beginning of the following week at 1272.50 for a profit of just over 10 per cent. As you can see from the chart, this move was another shake-out and the market swiftly reversed direction and went back up just as it had done back in 1998. However, I wanted no further part as I was now convinced this increased volatility coupled with the public stock market euphoria was a classic stage three ending. Therefore, I ignored the next entry signal (F), which occurred on the week ending 12 November.

Postscript – the market actually rallied a further 12 per cent before peaking in the middle of 2000, whereupon it began a well-documented bear market that, as I write this book, is now in its fifth year.

I'm afraid not all the investment trends I participate in are as consistent or as profitable as this example. The bull market in the S&P 500 was a strong trend and one that required very little analytical input until the end. This is often the case with powerful investment trends. The hard bit is getting in and getting out; the middle of a trend is fairly easy to manage and ironically it's also where you'll achieve the greatest profits. Personally, I've no idea whether the commodity bull market is going to be as easy to participate in as this example, but one thing I am convinced of is the tremendous potential commodities have to offer astute investors over the next decade.

6

Commodities – the next investment boom

Commodities in stage one

The point of investing is not to guess the future, but to act on new information before the whole world pounces on the idea.

Todd Buchholz

Commodities are now in the first stage of what will be a massive bull market and, to prove that we're at this stage of the cycle, a stage characterized by an apparent apathy to an investment or market that is already providing fantastic returns, let me recount a recent shopping trip. To obtain further research for this book, I went to the largest bookshop in the biggest shopping centre in Europe to purchase some books relating to commodities and the growth of the Asian economies. The business and finance section of the bookshop contained some 400-plus titles including *How to Be a Property Millionaire, Retire Rich with Property, The Buy-to-Let Bible, Buying to Rent: The key to your financial freedom, Property Ladder: How to make pounds from property, Profit from Property*, plus many more dealing with the subject of investing in property, yet there wasn't a single book on commodities, and the only book I could find on the phenomenal growth in Asia was published in 2001 and bore the interesting title *The Coming Collapse of China*. And that was it. This apathy towards the commodity story is a massive stage one signal considering the fantastic economic growth rates of China, India and Pakistan and the fact that commodity prices in general have already rallied over 80 per cent in the last three and a half years.

Another example that commodities are out of fashion despite their rising values comes from the 'professionals' of the fund management industry. Until recently, a fund manager who used alternative financial instruments such as futures and options was commonly known as a CTA, which stood for 'commodity trading adviser'. However, over the last few years, they have decided to rename themselves 'derivative fund managers' or 'hedge fund managers', dropping any reference to unfashionable commodities.

In fairness, the reason for this apathy is obvious when you realize that, over the 22 years to 2002, commodities on an inflation-adjusted basis did nothing but go down in value and it was virtually impossible for anyone to make any decent profits from participating in them. Even the commodity producers themselves either scaled down or completely closed their operations.

You may wonder why it's important that the common consensus needs to be so apathetic about an investment in stage one of its cycle. Essentially, the premise is that 'people talk their book' and if individuals or institutions are bullish on an investment then they already have a market position. Therefore, if very few are bullish, then very few have invested and this means that any recent price rally is more credible as it is likely to be the result of a supply/demand imbalance rather than pure speculation. It also indicates that there are still plenty of uncommitted investors who will eventually participate in the market at a later stage of its development, pushing prices even higher.

Having personally participated in both of the most recent investment booms, namely in technology 'dot.com' stocks and property, I can see the same attitudes towards commodities now that were held about these investments at the beginning of their trends. Remember how nobody wanted to own technology stocks in 1994 as the Nasdaq began to rally, compared with how many were participating in 2000 when that market collapsed. Another example occurred back in 1994. With the newspapers still full of tales about negative equity and repossessions, I had identified what I felt was a good case for the potential growth of residential property prices. They had just begun to emerge from a horrible bear market that had forced many to abandon property as a viable investment and, despite the fact that rental yields were strong and values were rising, residential property was still very much out of fashion. As I already owned my own home, I felt the best way for me to participate in this potential boom was to purchase some additional properties and rent them out. My target was to hold a portfolio of about 20 flats and to part-finance their acquisition I approached my bank for funding. My intention was to part-mortgage each property, with the rental income I received from my tenants covering the mortgage payments. This type of investment strategy is known today as 'buy to let' and there are now numerous lenders competing to lend to thousands of new investors who have 'just' realized this investment exists. Back in 1994, however, things were very different and my bank, with which I had an extremely good and long-standing relationship, declined to lend any funds secured against investment property. They explained that, owing to the recent decline in property values over the last few years and the resultant bad publicity incurred, property, especially residential, was the last place anyone should consider investing. Six months later, I made another application supported by a detailed business plan, and again my proposal was rejected. To be fair to my bank, they were not alone. At the time, nobody had a good word to say about residential property and yet prices had already begun to rally. Finally, 18 months later, in the summer of 1996, I was able to find another lender to finance my property purchases, which even drew the attention of the national press:

> Mr Shipman is spending between £55,000 to £60,000 each on one and two-bedroom flats and is expecting an annual gross yield of 11 to 14 per cent. 'I am looking mainly for capital appreciation with the rent covering my borrowing, maintenance and the letting fees'. Mr Shipman borrowed between 60 and 70 per cent of the purchase price from lenders Mortgage Trust and plans to repay the loans from rental income.
>
> *The Times*, 9 April 1997

Interestingly at the time, my bank's negativity towards my proposed property investments confirmed to me that we were in stage one of the boom. Conversely, in early 2003, when the same bank that had continually refused to back me then offered to take over my entire portfolio and provide additional funding to purchase more properties,

I took this as a confirming signal that property had now entered stage three of its cycle and promptly put all the 21 flats in my investment portfolio up for sale.

In summary, despite the odd reference to the price of oil on television and in the newspapers, commodity coverage and participation is still very low. This is significant considering the tremendous rally already under way in a number of commodity markets. For example, how much 'editorial' have you seen devoted to the recent gains of the following markets?

■ Coffee up 110 per cent in 18 months!
■ Sugar up 80 per cent in 12 months!
■ Lumber up 44 per cent in 5 months!
■ Copper up 105 per cent in 18 months!

At the moment, commodities just aren't sexy enough. The investment community and the investing public are still too preoccupied with property or hoping for a new stock market rally. Whilst this continues, we know we're still in stage one of the cycle, and the lower the number of participants at the beginning the stronger the investment trend will eventually be. These markets are moving up and yet nobody cares. That, my friends, is stage one – the best time to invest!

But aren't commodities risky?

Since I began my investing career back in the 1980s, there has always been a negative consensus of opinion towards commodities. Often viewed as risky and highly speculative, especially when compared to such 'sophisticated' investments as property, bonds and the stock market, many so-called professionals smirk when you mention they're in your portfolio. Personally, I see no difference between participating in sugar or wheat and participating in any other investment instrument. In my view, if they present an opportunity to make money, then they should be considered.

I like to keep my options open. In fact, over the last 20 or so years, despite the lack of any major long-term trends, commodities have rewarded me with some excellent profits and, with the recent publication of an in-depth academic study, you don't just have to take my word for it. The paper, titled *Facts and Fantasies about Commodity Futures*, was published by the Yale International Center for Finance in June 2004 and its authors, professors Gary Gorton of the University of Pennsylvania and the National Bureau of Economic Research and K Geert Rouwenhorst of the Yale School of Management, present an extremely thorough review of the performance of commodities and how they compare to stocks and bonds. Their conclusions are detailed in the following abstract from the study:

> We construct an equally-weighted index of commodity futures monthly returns over the period between July of 1959 and March of 2004 in order to study simple properties of commodity futures as an asset class. Fully-collateralized commodity futures have historically offered the same return and Sharpe ratio as equities. While the risk premium on commodity futures is essentially the same as equities, commodity futures returns are negatively correlated with equity returns and bond returns. The negative correlation between commodity futures and the other asset classes is due, in significant part, to different behavior over the business cycle. In addition, commodity futures are positively correlated with inflation, unexpected inflation, and changes in expected inflation.

This confirms my own personal experience that commodities are no riskier an investment than property, bonds or the stock market. Also, they can move counter-cyclical to trends in other asset classes and they offer a better hedge against that enemy of everyone's savings and lifestyle – inflation. On the subject of inflation, the study states: 'Commodity Futures have an opposite exposure to inflation compared to Stocks and Bonds. Stocks and Bonds are negatively correlated with inflation, while the correlation of Commodity Futures with inflation is positive at all horizons.' Also, further studies, conducted by the Commodity Research Bureau, confirm how major trend changes in commodity values have consistently preceded similar changes in the Consumer Price Index figure and often acted as a leading indicator of interest rate yields. This evidence for the long-term benefit of an asset allocation to commodities is further enhanced if you factor in the current and future supply/demand imbalance for most raw materials.

Why commodity prices are moving higher

Major long-term market trends are the result of a shift in the supply/demand balance. Whatever the reason, if supply exceeds demand prices go down, and if demand exceeds supply prices go up. Usually you will find that most trends are the result of a shift in one of these economic drivers. However, when both demand rises and supply shrinks, you can expect massive trends that exceed all early price forecasts and historical comparisons. Commodities are now in that type of market condition. For reasons I will shortly explain, we have a 'double whammy' of dwindling supply coupled with an explosive and sustainable increase in demand. In addition, owing to the supply logistics of most commodities, this imbalance cannot be reconciled quickly, thereby creating the opportunity for a very long and rewarding bull market.

The demand story

The Global Village

To provide you with a more basic example of how the supply/demand imbalance in commodities has been created, let's look at this little tale. Imagine for a moment that the entire world is just one village, the Global Village.

Once upon a time, this village consisted of shops and businesses selling goods and services to the village's inhabitants, who in turn worked in the industries that supplied these goods and services. This village, however, was divided into two distinct halves. In the Western part lived the 'moderately well off to rich' inhabitants. They had well-paid jobs, drove cars, watched television, used mobile phones and ate fine food. It was they who earned the majority of the money. In the Eastern part of the village, however, it was a different story. Although a similar percentage of the population lived there, they were much poorer by comparison. Very few had televisions or cars and, in fact, some didn't even have electricity and lived in wooden huts. To eat, they had to grow their own food for they could not afford to go to the shops and, although they were very hard-working, their income was minuscule when compared to that of those in the Western part of the village. This had been the status quo for centuries and, because the shopkeepers and other service providers knew they sold the vast majority of their goods and services to the residents in the West, they maintained their inventories accordingly, ensuring they had just enough to meet the consistent demand from the West.

Then, all of a sudden, things began to change. Some bright spark living in the West realized that, because the residents in the East lived so cheaply, they would be happy to manufacture the West's goods for less wages than those of the current employees, who lived in the more affluent and expensive West. Gradually, more and more businesses realized the huge potential of this cheap and untapped labour on the other side of the village and it wasn't long before everyone was looking to invest in the East. With that investment came improved infrastructure – roads, electricity and better living conditions. Before long, many residents and workers from the East were earning enough money to begin purchasing some of the luxuries that their Western counterparts had become accustomed to years ago.

Suddenly, the shopkeepers and service providers became inundated with the new Eastern demand for their products. They asked farmers to supply more meat and vegetables; they asked manufacturers to produce more cars, bikes and televisions; they even needed hundreds more mobile phones; but there was a problem. Manufacturers, farmers and other producers couldn't simply step up production to meet this ever-growing demand. They just didn't have the infrastructure. For too many years, they had profited handsomely from a fairly steady demand for their goods and there hadn't been any incentive to spend these profits on providing infrastructure to produce surplus inventory. In fact, they had streamlined their businesses so well that it would now take many years before they could even hope to meet this new demand from the East.

The price of anything that is the subject of strong demand but for which there is only a limited supply will carry a large premium, and this inflated cost will remain until supply and demand can once again achieve equilibrium.

To turn this little story from fiction to fact, simply replace the word 'village' with 'world'.

Introducing China

There are a number of key factors driving the current gains in commodity prices but none is more influential or more likely to grow stronger than the demand from the 'Middle Kingdom', China. This nation of over 1.3 billion people (with 300 million under the age of 20) accounts for a continually rising share of the worldwide demand for every raw material and consumable commodity. China is the world's most populous country, with a continuous culture dating back over 4,000 years, and many of the elements that have contributed to the evolution of civilization originated in China, from paper and gunpowder through to credit banking and paper money. It is not so much a new emerging country but more like an old superpower regaining its place as the world's most influential nation.

The second Industrial Revolution

Following many years under a strict regime, its leaders, whilst not abandoning their core political beliefs, have cleverly utilized a vast low-cost labour force to manufacture and export the nation's way to prosperity and help China finally take its rightly deserved place in the world order. Already China is manufacturing over $60 billion worth of consumer electronics a year, far more than Western Europe and, in just a few years, the number of registered businesses in China has grown from 90,000 to over 3 million. This is a tried-and-tested route to kick-starting economic activity and has been used successfully in the past by countries such as Japan, Malaysia and Taiwan. It is nigh on impossible for the Western nations to match China's low-cost manufacturing because on pure labour costs alone the advantage is enormous, with the average Chinese worker earning just £177 a year compared to over £22,000 for a Western counterpart.

There are numerous examples with strong statistical and anecdotal evidence that illustrate the advances China is making and the effect this is having upon the commodity markets, and in the following pages I would like to identify some of them. They are in no particular order but all are of equal importance and I think you will find they make a compelling case for a boom in commodity values.

The current modernization of China is equivalent to that of the West just after the Second World War and, although some 'experts' question whether China can maintain the 2004 growth rate of 9.5 per cent, they have failed to recognize that it was consistent with the performance of the past 25 years. Yes, for over a quarter of a century, China's average growth rate has been in excess of 9 per cent per annum. It is this sustained growth that has enabled the country to emerge from a poverty-stricken condition where a great famine killed nearly 40 million people between 1959 and 1961 to become one of the world's most influential economies. Deng Xiaoping, the patriarch who set China on this economic course, supposedly said it is 'glorious to grow rich' and this has now become the mantra for many thousands of China's new entrepreneurs and business people.

The world's largest consumer

By the fourth quarter 2004, China was already the world's number one consumer of iron ore, steel, copper, platinum and soybeans and the number two consumer of oil and energy-related products. It is also importing large quantities of cotton, gold, silver, lead, aluminium and nickel. Even the outlook for zinc has changed, as China recently moved from being a net exporter to net importer for the first time in over 15 years.

Because of its size, everything China does is on a large scale even though the percentage of participation within the country itself may be small. For example, China is not a coffee-drinking nation and, in fact, per capita consumption of coffee is 50 times less than that of Switzerland but, because of the sheer size of its population, China is already a bigger consumer of world coffee production. Another example is jewellery. Although the majority of the population live in rural areas in conditions that can at best be described as less than affluent and there is only a small percentage of its citizens with any disposable income, China is already consuming more than 50 per cent of the world's entire platinum production for use in jewellery. What's going to happen to the demand and price of coffee, platinum and other similar commodities as China's continued growth enables more and more of its population to afford and enjoy Western-style living and luxuries? Already the smart, exclusive hotels and restaurants of Shanghai and Beijing are full of affluent people sporting exclusive Western designer brands, and the fashionable shopping malls in the big cities are full to the brim with imported luxury goods. To give you a feel for how much new demand could be just around the corner, it is estimated that in the next decade rural reform will create 800 million new Chinese consumers. That's approximately 14 per cent of the world's entire population and nearly three times more than the entire population of the United States.

Add that new demand to a country that is, in 2005, already responsible for the following consumption facts and you have a level of demand unheard of in history:

■ China is already the world's biggest consuming country according to a report issued recently by the Earth Policy Institute.

■ Its factories and homes currently burn 40 per cent more coal than the United States.

■ China is the world's largest consumer of refrigerators.

■ It has the highest number of households with digital televisions in the world.

■ China is the largest consumer of mobile telephones, with two of its network providers, China Mobile and China Unicom, in the top three largest mobile phone companies in the world. Their combined number of subscribers is already more than two and a half times greater than that of Vodaphone, yet less than 20 per cent of China's population actually owns a mobile.

■ The number of personal computers in China is doubling every two years and this must have had a contributing factor in the recent Chinese purchase of IBM's PC division for $1.75 billion.

■ Although only a tiny percentage of the population can drive or even afford a car, there is already a waiting list for Bentleys, the top-of-the-range luxury car, despite a price tag of nearly £400,000 (double the European retail price).

■ China is the biggest market for BMW's top-of-the-range 7 Series.

■ Volkswagen already sells more cars in China than it does in its German homeland.

And perhaps the most visual sign of the change to China's social and economic status and its development as a consuming nation comes from Tiananmen Square. Many of you will recall the memorable image of a lone student standing in protest in front of an advancing tank. Well, this same location now boasts a different symbol just a few hundred yards from the mausoleum of Chairman Mao – a Porsche car showroom!

Comrade Mickey

To illustrate further how China's communist regime is relaxing its once strict prohibitions, consider this interesting alliance recently covered in a Fortune 500 magazine article. Walt Disney was proud to announce it had teamed up with the 70 million-member Chinese Communist Youth League to promote reading skills. Instead of just reading *The Thoughts of Chairman Mao*, these children, still bedecked in their communist red uniforms, are now also privy to the collective wisdom of Winnie-the-Pooh, Piglet and Roo! Disney's motive is obvious: with over 290 million children under the age of 14, China offers tremendous growth potential for merchandising, something the world's second-largest media and entertainment conglomerate is particularly good at. Disney's *The Lion King* was the first foreign film ever released in China and already Chinese television regularly broadcasts *The Dragon Club*, a half-hour show combining Disney programming with short segments produced in China. To boost their Chinese strategy further, autumn 2005 sees the opening of Hong Kong Disneyland on Lantau Island complete with Sleeping Beauty's castle and Main Street.

Shipping

Just off the coast of Newcastle, Australia sits a human-made spectacle that's fast becoming a local tourist attraction. People have taken to driving to a lookout point just to witness its sheer size.

What is it? A queue of empty bulk freight ships moored at anchor waiting for their turn to sail in and collect the coal needed for the power plants of north-east Asia. On average there are over 30 vessels and on one occasion there were over 50. The reason for this seagoing traffic jam is that the coal these ships carry cannot be supplied fast enough to meet the demand. The massive growth of China is placing a tremendous strain upon the infrastructure of the producing nations. The same ships that sit off the coast of Australia, or at iron ore ports in India and Brazil, must also line up again for as long as three weeks to unload their cargo at the heavily congested Chinese ports. These shipping bottlenecks are responsible for incapacitating as much as 20 per cent of the bulk freighters in the world and, in under 12 months, have more than doubled the cost of moving freight.

To arrest this problem, shipyards around the world are building at full capacity but not only does the world need more freighters but it also needs the shipyards to build them. Even China itself is building dozens of new shipyards, including the world's largest in Shanghai. Although recent statistics show that global ship orders have more than doubled in number, these ships won't be seen on the high seas immediately, meaning the worldwide shipping shortage will remain for the foreseeable future. The strong demand from China for electricity will not go away either. Once they've got used to all those toasters, televisions and air-conditioners they will only want more and more. In 2004 alone, China added 45 gigawatts of power-generating capacity, which is equivalent to the entire capacity of Australia!

In short, we have a shipping crisis. The world needs more freighters because China's strong growth is tying up the majority of the existing fleet. However, the shipyards can't get the steel they need because there aren't enough ships to move the ore to the steel plants. Add to that the fact that many of the world's oil tankers will have to be scrapped soon because they do not conform to the tough new ecological regulations and we have another crisis that will send raw material prices even higher.

Steptoe and Son

Those of you based in the UK may remember the TV comedy *Steptoe and Son*, which was broadcast on the BBC. The series followed the exploits of a father-and-son 'rag and bone' business. For those who don't know, this term applied to people who used to drive around town in horse-drawn carts or old lorries collecting unwanted rubbish from residents. Typically, the rubbish consisted of old beds, washing machines, toasters – anything that had a second-hand scrap value. In fact, there was even a famous old musical song about this profession, with its title based upon the rag and bone merchant's street cry, 'Any old iron'. They would then sell this 'rubbish' to various scrap metal merchants for small amounts of money. It was a meagre existence and these individuals typically lived just above the poverty line. It was this predicament and the fact that Steptoe Junior always had delusions of grandeur, craving a more affluent and respectable lifestyle, that made this TV comedy such a success.

Now, let me tell you about how the current demand for raw materials has turned John Neu, a modern-day US 'rag and bone man', into a multimillionaire. He lives not far from the hub of New York's financial district and, just like Steptoe and Son, he collects unwanted scrap – radiators, televisions, bedsprings, toasters, old bikes and cars, etc. If it's metal and you don't want it, he does. Neu takes this rubbish and sells it around the world, and guess whose appetite for all things metal is so insatiable it will happily pay for the United States' cast-offs? Yes, China. In fact, demand is so strong that scrap metal prices have rallied over 400 per cent from $57 a gross ton to over $300 in just a few years. This is further proof of the effect that China's rapid growth is having upon the cost of basic raw materials. As far as TV comedy series go, if *Steptoe and Son* had to be remade now, it would look more like *The Beverly Hillbillies*!

Construction boom

The demand for building materials is set to grow even further as the world's most populous nation undertakes a massive urbanization process. Whole sections of China's metropolitan areas have been transformed into building sites with Beijing, the nation's capital and home to over 14 million people, seeing the kind of construction boom that usually occurs following a war. This £42 billion programme is due in part to the forthcoming 2008 Olympics but is also symbolic of China's nationwide regeneration. In Shanghai, already home to a fifth of the world's construction cranes, the new World Financial Centre is going to be the tallest building in the world and, not far away from the city, work has begun on a British-style satellite city with the interesting name of Thames Town. This building boom is set to continue over the next few years, as 400 million rural Chinese move into urban areas and, to facilitate this relocation, it is estimated that China will have to build three cities the size of London each year for the next three decades.

Even outside the urban areas, in addition to hundreds of new bridges and motorways, there are enormous construction and engineering projects in progress. One such project is the Three Gorges Dam, which when completed will be China's largest construction since the Great Wall. Its hydropower turbines will be so large they will create electricity equivalent to the output generated from over 14 nuclear power plants.

Education

There are currently over a thousand universities in China providing nearly 2 million new graduates to the labour force each year. They are extremely hard-working individuals prepared to work over 100 hours per week, and over a third of these are engineers for China's urbanization programme. These students go straight into the workforce; 'gap' years don't exist. Another interesting statistic revealed recently on television is that the number of Chinese currently learning English is greater than the entire population of the United States.

The secret growth weapon – the overseas Chinese

Everything I've documented so far illustrates the size and power of China and its large population, but there is another hitherto unconsidered group who are forcing the pace of growth even further – the overseas Chinese.

Many years ago following centuries of poverty, hundreds of thousands if not millions of Chinese left their homeland in search of work and prosperity. They travelled and settled all over the world and, at the time, their labour was significant in the growth of many Western economies. For example, the construction of the United States' railways in the 19th century was heavily reliant upon Chinese labour, and many Western cities from New York to London have a 'China Town' where these immigrants finally settled and rekindled their culture. In fact, over 90 per cent of the 57 million overseas Chinese are now naturalized citizens of their adopted countries. As well as being extremely hard workers, the overseas Chinese are also very astute businesspeople, and you may be surprised to learn that if their financial clout were grouped together they would be the third-biggest economy in the world.

In short, their influence is phenomenal. For example, in Indonesia, Thailand and the Philippines, although they represent less than 4 per cent of the population, the overseas Chinese control over 70 per cent of the wealth. Recently they have turned their attention to investing their wealth back into their motherland, China, and recent statistics show that the overseas Chinese account for 80 per cent of all foreign investment and own 90 per cent of all small and mid-size Asian companies. Such is the scale of their investment that it has helped China recently surpass the United States as the largest recipient of direct foreign investment.

No ecological restrictions

Another positive factor for continued growth is that, despite being one of the largest manufacturing countries in the world and also the world's largest consumer of most raw materials, China is categorized under the Kyoto Protocol as a developing nation. This means it remains exempt from the fossil fuel consumption restrictions that control the activity of most nations. So, at present, the Chinese can continue to expand at will without the ecological restrictions that curb similar growth in other nations.

China – the risks

Nothing in life and especially investing is completely clear cut and risk free. Although I firmly believe China will continue to grow and suck up any available supply for commodities, thereby creating massive bull markets, it would be imprudent of me to ignore some of the risks that may sabotage my long-term view or, at least, provide a few nasty hiccups. The leadership of President Hu Jintao and Prime Minister Wen Jiabao has the difficult task of maintaining China's spectacular return to the world order in a manner that benefits all of its citizens. Inequality across a population is a common problem, be it the north–south divide in Britain or the wealth disparity between China's rural poor and the more affluent urban dwellers. This type of problem will always exist but the target for the Chinese leadership is to reduce this gap and bring more balance between the 'haves' and the 'have-nots'. This, I'm sure, they will eventually accomplish but it won't happen quickly.

Fortunately, although the rebirth of China is a great story, it is thankfully not a new one, and we can learn a lot from the history of other nations that have followed a similar path. The past is a good teacher about the potential hazards to following an investment strategy heavily reliant upon such economic growth, and the one abiding theme as past economies grew is that nothing goes in a straight line and there are always many setbacks along the way. Progress is never smooth. The United States is a good example when it enjoyed its tremendous growth between 1800 and the early 1900s. It industrialized at a phenomenal rate and yet during the same period also experienced a civil war and numerous financial crises. Did that stop the United States from becoming a superpower? No, and the same will be true of China.

In conclusion, there could be possible economic and political crises but China's trend towards becoming a superpower and one of the world's leading economies will continue unabated. This view is shared by the International Monetary Fund, which despite recently warning that China's spectacular growth could lead to economic problems also stated that they would have a 'relatively short-term impact' if they occurred.

Introducing India

To compound the demand story even further, China is not the only major nation mobilizing its economy and workforce. There are others, the largest of which is India. The Indus Valley civilization is one of the oldest in the world, dating back over 5,000 years. Since then the land has been subjected to numerous invasions and incursions, from Aryan tribes around 1500 BC through to British colonization, which ended in 1947 when India achieved independence. With a population of nearly 1.1 billion people, it is one of the most populous nations on the planet, second only to China. In addition, it is the largest democracy in the world and has English as its national, political and commercial language, which is a tremendous asset to international trade. Combining India's large and highly intellectual population with an increase in investment from overseas will enable it to join China as one of the most powerful and influential economies in the world.

A service industry-led expansion

As a collective group of people, India's population ranks as one of the best in the world in terms of intellectual ability. Owing, it would seem, to a combination of inherent natural ability and a strong educational ethic, it is no coincidence that four of the 10 biggest universities in the world are in India. This provides the country with possibly its most important resource and one that it has harvested well through the outsourcing of information technology services. Capitalizing on its large number of well-educated, highly skilled people has enabled this once poor nation to move towards a more positive and affluent future. In fact, information technology has expanded so quickly that India now plays host to most of the world's major computer hardware and software companies. Indian computer engineers and software writers have proved themselves as competent as their Western counterparts whilst exhibiting a stronger work ethic and costing less than a tenth in salaries and bonuses. However, it's not just software and call-centre services that are booming. India also has a number of other rapidly expanding high-tech industries, covering car components, aviation, satellites, automation controls and life sciences. Figures show that outsourcing generated more than $7 billion in revenue in 2003 and it is widely expected this figure will have doubled by 2007 and will double again by 2012. Just as China is regarded as the world's low-cost manufacturer, India is now regarded as the world's low-cost service provider.

East goes West

In 1995, just four years after India opened its economy to outsiders, Kentucky Fried Chicken opened its first outlet. Initially the target of Hindu nationalists and other sympathizers who saw this as the beginning of an infiltration of the evil and corrupt capitalist West, the Bangalore-based 'restaurant' appeared destined for a short life. However, it survived and within the next nine years KFC's parent, Yum Brands, opened a further 100 KFC and Pizza Hut outlets. They expect to have over 1,000 restaurants operational by 2014. Ironically, just as people in Britain crave the spicy and exotic Indian curries that now form the cornerstone of the nation's diet, so middle-class Indians now crave the Western flavours incorporated into the chicken drumsticks and cheese feast pizzas sold by these establishments. The *New York Times* recently reported on how, the day after an Indian festival where the traditional cuisine is vegetarian, consumers converged on their local Pizza Hut, ordering pizza with non-vegetarian toppings. Just as the affluent Chinese have begun to enjoy Western-style consumables, so the Indian population is following suit. Rolex, Armani, Gucci, Reebok, Adidas, Nokia, Coca-Cola, Pepsi and Mercedes, to name but a few, have all entered the Indian marketplace capitalizing not only upon the desire for Western status symbols but also upon the fact that the Indian middle classes are growing in number at a phenomenal rate. Despite a strong cultural heritage and rich history of tradition, India and its people are embracing Western tastes and, as the new wealth filters down to the majority of the population, who still reside below the poverty line, this demand for consumables is set to grow even stronger.

Fast-improving infrastructure

India's Commerce Minister, Arun Jaitley, recently confirmed that the country is currently in the middle of the largest highway construction programme in the world. Identifying the importance of how an improved infrastructure will help India become a developed nation by 2020, he also confirmed that the construction industry is in the process of acquiring the latest skills and technologies. The aim is to help villages gain an urban infrastructure whilst the big cities themselves will benefit from facelifts that will add metros, business centres and underground parking facilities. There is now a frenzy of construction activity unparalleled in the history of the country in terms of scale, complexity and quality. Shopping centres and multiplex cinemas, previously unheard of in India, are now appearing in every town and city, allowing Indian consumers to enjoy the same shopping, dining and entertainment experience as their Western counterparts. In addition, the smoked glass, steel and marble finishes that are commonplace throughout the world's business centres are now appearing in the commercial areas of India's major cities. There are also entire new towns and cities being planned from scratch to cater for India's successful new business entrepreneurs. For example, the Sahara Lake City near

Mumbai will attempt to offer its inhabitants the 'world's best living'. Currently, India lags way behind China and the rest of the world in basic steel consumption but, as the benefits of its outsourcing boom now filter through the economy, the demand is already growing.

India's commodity demand

Although India benefits from a number of natural resources including iron ore, natural gas and diamonds in addition to holding the fourth-largest coal reserves in the world, it is also a major commodity consumer. It is already the world's largest consumer of both silver and gold, and is responsible for importing about a third of the world's entire annual production. It is already the world's fourth-largest consumer of crude oil, and in 2004 alone its oil consumption grew by 11 per cent despite sky-high prices. In fact, India has now emerged as China's main rival in grabbing oil contracts from as many countries as possible. It has yet to wield the same influence over other commodities as its Asian neighbour but, with a population of over 1 billion and an outstanding growth rate, it is only a matter of time before India catches up.

In conclusion, as with China the majority of India's population still live below the poverty line and it will take many years before the slums disappear. However, the pace of change has already been swift and India's growth rates demand respect with an average of nearly 7 per cent per annum over the last 10 years. Combined with an economy boosted by large amounts of tax receipts, a surplus in the international balance of payments, a high investment rate and more than $130 billion in foreign exchange reserves (excluding gold), it is as important to our commodity demand story as China. Confirmation of this growing status appeared in a report recently issued by Deutsche Bank predicting that India will be the world's third-largest economy by 2020.

Introducing Pakistan

Another major future source of commodity demand comes from neighbouring Pakistan. Of the world's 10 most populous nations, only China has a greater rate of growth than the Islamic Republic of Pakistan, a nation of over 160 million potential consumers. In 1947, British

India divided to create the largely Hindu India and the Muslim state of Pakistan. This led to two major conflicts between the nations over the disputed territory of Kashmir and, in 1971, following a third war with India, East Pakistan became the separate nation of Bangladesh. Although the dispute over Kashmir has yet to be satisfactorily resolved, tensions have eased as both India and Pakistan pursue a more diplomatic route. This in turn has enabled Pakistan's leadership to focus its attention on economic growth, with the resulting effect that the $110 billion economy is now recognized as a serious player amongst the evolving nations. Recent figures announced by Prime Minister Shauhat Aziz show that Pakistan expected its economy to have grown by over 8 per cent in the year ended 30 June 2005, and the leadership is targeting a similar rate of growth for the next 12 months. Whether it can sustain such a phenomenal expansion has been questioned but I believe the trend is definitely now set. Pakistan is growing fast and, as with China and India, this growth increases the demand for all raw materials. Although it is a major exporter of raw cotton and has extensive natural gas reserves, Pakistan will still need to import large quantities of almost all the other major commodities.

Pakistan has been an impoverished and underdeveloped country suffering from the many years of internal political disputes and expensive confrontations with neighbouring India. However, bolstered by overseas investment and improved internal policies, it is now making rapid progress. Following a similar export-led programme to China and tapping into the vast amount of cheap labour available have already led to a solid economic recovery over the last three years. Continued expansion for a nation that already boasts a population greater than that of Germany and France combined sets it up to play an important role in the commodity demand story.

Summary of the demand story

All this information represents the condition of these nations as I write the copy for this book but, such is their speed of change and improvement, this information can only be, at best, a snapshot. Their growth is accelerating every day and, therefore, any statistics are dated the moment they're written. Anyhow, I'm sure you get the idea – whatever I've written here, it will be bigger and better by the time you read it!

These nations are going to be *the* major influence in the world over the next 50 years. We are in the early stages of a unique shift of power back from the West to the East. Civilization is returning to its roots and, whilst this change isn't always going to run smoothly, it will continue regardless. Ironically, at the moment, China, India and Pakistan all to some degree rely upon the West to purchase their exports and outsource for technical expertise as well as providing much-needed investment capital. However, this will not last for ever and the heavily debt-laden Western economies, in particular those of the United States and Europe, will then be at the mercy of these newly emerging Eastern superpowers. As far as we are concerned, this is all in the distant future. What matters now and over the next few years is how we, as investors, can profit from the growth of these nations whose combined population totals over 2.6 billion people and represents 40 per cent of the world's entire population.

I think investing in the individual countries or their stock markets is best left to those who have the expertise and possess an intimate local knowledge. A far safer strategy, and it's the one I personally use for my own money and I'm also recommending you consider via this book, would be to invest in what China, India and Pakistan need and have to buy for themselves – commodities. By using the strategies suggested in this book you will be participating indirectly in the growth of these nations but safe in the knowledge that your money is held by a UK-regulated company and can be accessed whenever you wish.

The supply story

Historically low commodity prices discouraging investment

> Your greatest investment opportunities come from industries where those who know them best, love them least, because they have been disappointed most.
>
> Donald Coxe

On an inflation-adjusted basis, commodity prices are cheap and remain at levels last seen during the Great Depression of the 1930s. With prices at such depressed levels, there has been no incentive for producers to maintain inventories or invest in new production technology. Being a producer of commodities has become an unglamorous occupation with low, unreliable and erratic profits. In the last couple of decades, why would people set out to make careers in farming, oil or mining when they could make their fortunes as IT specialists, estate agents or investment bankers? While investors and businesspeople were pouring their money into technology stocks and property, no one really gave a thought to investing in oil exploration, mining or sowing a coffee or sugar plantation. This lack of interest and under-investment has been vividly illustrated by the sharp reduction in the number of participants and the amount of capacity available – husbandry is neglected, mines are closed, exploration budgets are cut and crops are substituted. Even my local farm, near where I grew up as a boy, has been transformed from a once thriving agricultural business in the 1960s and 1970s into two golf courses!

When commodity prices are low, new production is discouraged, as production without profit is financial suicide in a free market economy. Therefore, overall production contracts and, if demand suddenly increases for whatever reason, the first commercially sound response from a producer is to sell any surplus inventory held. With the odd exception, this has been the way most producers of raw materials have dealt with the recent increases in demand, and in the short term this tactic usually works fine. Demand is met without having to break sweat and invest in new production. However, if demand continues to increase, as is happening now, producers are faced with a problem. After decades of little or no investment, most now lack the infrastructure simply to step up production, and this problem does not have a quick fix. For example, it takes many years to grow a coffee plant from seed to a stage of maturity where it can produce coffee beans and, similarly, reopening a closed mine or smelt is not a project that can be undertaken quickly. In short, the commodity markets are not capable of quickly meeting a sustained rise in demand. This is in stark contrast to the stock market, where increases in demand for shares can be quickly met by simply issuing more of them. For commodities, new supply takes time, plants need to grow, fruit needs to ripen, minerals need to be mined and, whilst the world waits, prices go up. In some cases, such as crude oil, the commodity is also finite and beginning to run out!

Where has all the oil gone?

Although there are still billions of barrels' worth of crude oil lying beneath the ground, the world is now consuming it at an alarming and ever-growing rate. It is not a commodity that can regenerate itself and, once it's gone, it's gone. Already more than 40 oil-producing countries around the world have passed their peak in the amount of oil they can produce. Here, in Europe, we reached our oil production peak in 2000; Indonesia (a member of OPEC) peaked in 1997; Iran (another OPEC member) peaked in 1974; Romania (once the target of Nazi Germany for oil production) peaked in 1976; and one of the world's largest and most influential oil producers, the former Soviet Union, hit its production peak nearly two decades ago in 1987. Furthermore, under-investment in oil exploration has led to a dwindling number of new discoveries.

Transportation problems will also affect supply

The importance of oil is also significant to the prices for other commodities when you factor in the cost of its use in the operation of machinery and transportation. In fact, there are also logistical problems with transportation that will cause higher commodity prices. Years of under-investment in the world's shipping fleet will sabotage any meaningful short-term increases in supply. For example, the oil tanker fleet is ageing and about to enter a period of phase-outs of the obsolete vessels. All pre-MARPOL (International Convention for the Prevention of Pollution from Ships, 1973, as modified by the Protocol, 1978) tankers must be scrapped and all single-hull MARPOL tankers must be phased out by 2010. With the global demand for crude oil climbing every year, the world needs a larger tanker fleet, not a smaller one, and yet until very recently the building of new eco-friendly vessels has been limited at best.

Strong demand + weak supply = higher prices

In conclusion, I believe the economic growth of China, India and Pakistan will continue to be a substantial force in the global economy for decades to come. Evidence of this growth is graphically detailed in the price movements of the commodity markets where the dynamics of supply and demand are most evident:

■ *Demand is strong.* The massive regeneration of the world's most heavily populated nations, whose combined populace totals nearly half of the world's entire population, has created an unquenchable thirst for almost every raw material on the planet.
■ *Supply is weak.* Years of under-investment and expensive environmental restrictions have kept commodity production at extremely low levels and, owing to the very nature of commodity supply, this shortage cannot be quickly addressed.
■ *The trend is up.* Strong demand and weak supply equal higher prices.

7

The commodity markets

The great thing about participating in commodities is that it's relatively easy to understand and relate to what you're investing in. They're not a highly valued IT company that's yet to show a profit; they're not a junk bond; they're not a long/short arbitrage hedge fund. Commodities are real, they're tangible and, wherever you're reading this book, you are surrounded by them. From the cup of coffee you're drinking to the cotton shirt, blouse, socks, underwear or leather shoes you're wearing to the chair you're sitting in and even the pages of this book, they're all commodities. Somebody produces them because somebody demands them and they all have a value.

The following is a brief overview of the most active commodity markets. They all have different qualities, different supply and production criteria and different demands and uses. Some have fascinating histories that date back beyond the dawn of civilization but they all have one thing in common – sooner or later they will come back into fashion and their respective values will soar. It seems as if commodities are the 'black sheep' of the investment family. This is wrong. They deserve your respect and your consideration both from the basis of absolute return and as a hedge against inflation.

Ignore them at your peril.

Aluminium

What is it?

Aluminium is the most abundant metallic element found in the world. The ancient Greeks and Romans used salts of this metal as dyeing mordants and for dressing wounds. Since it was first discovered, aluminium has been extremely difficult to separate from rock and it is still the world's most difficult metal to recover despite being the most common. First isolated in 1825, it wasn't until 1886 that the first practical process for producing this silvery, lightweight metal was discovered and, today, electrolytic reduction is still the primary method.

Who produces it?

The world's largest producers of aluminium are China, Russia, the United States and Canada.

What is it used for?

Aluminium's excellent strength-to-weight ratio makes it very popular in the construction of automobiles, boat hulls, railway carriages and aircraft. In addition, because of its high heat conductivity, it is used to make the pistons of the internal combustion engine as well as cooking equipment. Aluminium is also used in low-temperature nuclear reactors owing to the fact that it absorbs very few neutrons.

Cocoa

What is it?

Cocoa is the name given to the powder derived from the seeds of the cacao tree, a tree that can take over five years to reach maturity but then live for another 45 years or more. Labelled by the Spanish over 500 years ago as 'the food of the gods', it still remains a commodity in strong demand. Essentially, cocoa comprises 40 per cent fat, 20 per cent protein and 40 per cent carbohydrate and also contains the stimulant theobromine, an alkaloid related to caffeine.

Who produces it?

Nearly half of the world's production is accounted for by the Ivory Coast with two other African nations, Ghana and Nigeria, supplying a further 20 per cent. Outside of Africa, the main producers are Brazil, Malaysia, Indonesia and the Dominican Republic.

What is it used for?

Originally used by the Aztecs as a drink, nowadays nearly two-thirds of cocoa bean production is used to make chocolate and chocolate-based products. It's still, in my humble opinion, 'the food of the gods'.

Coffee

What is it?

As a cash commodity it is the second most valuable in the world. The coffee tree is actually a tropical evergreen shrub but it has the potential to grow to 100 feet tall. It grows in the regions between the Tropics of Cancer and Capricorn, where it requires and receives year-round warm temperatures combined with a plentiful amount of rainfall. Coffee is classified into two types of beans: arabica, which is the most widely produced representing nearly 70 per cent of world production, and robusta, which is grown at lower altitudes and has a stronger flavour.

Who produces it?

Behind the obvious leader in world production, Brazil, you might be surprised to learn that the second-biggest coffee grower is Vietnam whose recent production numbers have knocked Colombia into third place. Indonesia is also another significant producer.

What is it used for?

Although wine was actually the first drink to be produced from coffee, we are now all familiar with the warm beverage made from the roasted coffee bean, be it a latte, cappuccino, mocha or espresso.

Copper

What is it?

Dating back over 10,000 years, copper is humankind's oldest metal, with its name derived from the Mediterranean island of Cyprus, which was originally the primary source of the metal. Copper is one of the most widely used industrial metals because of its many varied qualities. It is an excellent conductor of electricity, has strong corrosion-resistant properties and is 'biostatic', which means that bacteria cannot grow on its surface, making it very attractive for hygienic applications such as food processing and air-conditioning equipment. In addition, it is also used to produce the alloys bronze (a copper–tin alloy) and brass (a copper–zinc alloy), both of which are actually stronger than the pure metal itself.

Who produces it?

Chile is the world's largest producer of copper and responsible for over a third of its supply, with the United States, Indonesia and Australia also accounting for significant output.

What is it used for?

Nearly three-quarters of copper demand relates to electrical products, particularly in relation to building and construction.

Corn

What is it?

Corn is a native grain of the American continents with fossils of its pollen found under Mexico City dating back over 80,000 years. A member of the grass family, it is a hardy plant capable of being grown at a wide variety of altitudes from sea level up to 12,000 feet, and it can also grow in areas with little natural water right up to tropical climates with extensive annual rainfall.

Who produces it?

The United States accounts for over 40 per cent of world corn production with China contributing a further 20 per cent. The next largest producers are Brazil and the European Union. Particularly important for the supply/demand argument of this book is the fact that China, despite being the world's second-largest producer, actually consumes more corn than it produces!

What is it used for?

Predominately as a feed for livestock. Other uses for corn include gasoline additives, adhesives, cooking oil, sweeteners, margarine and food for humans.

Cotton

What is it?

Used by humans for many thousands of years and in particular by the ancient civilizations of China, India and Egypt, cotton is a vegetable fibre grown naturally from small trees and shrubs. It requires stable conditions of sunshine and water during its growth season and then a dry period for harvesting, which can make it extremely vulnerable to changes in weather patterns.

Who produces it?

The world's largest cotton producers, namely China, India, Pakistan and the United States, are also the world's largest consumers, which can lead to very tight supply/demand margins during periods of poor crop production.

What is it used for?

It is used in a wide range of products from clothing and linen to medical supplies.

Crude oil

What is it?

Crude oil, also known as 'black gold' to many commodity players, was formed many millions of years ago from the decayed remains of tiny aquatic life. Believed to have medicinal properties by many ancient civilizations, it was also used as an adhesive for the building of ships and the making of weapons and jewellery. The pyramids were held together by it, as were the great walls of Babylon. Until the invention of the kerosene lamp in 1854, most oil discoveries made by prospectors drilling for water or brine were met with dismay. The Industrial Revolution and the subsequent advances made during the 20th century changed this perception of oil for ever. Today, it is the single-largest product in world trade.

Who produces it?

The world's largest producers of oil are Saudi Arabia, Russia, Norway, the United States, Iran, China, Mexico, Venezuela and Indonesia although, as widely documented, the United States, China and Indonesia all now consume more oil than they produce!

What is it used for?

Various grades of crude oil from the heavy 'sour' crude to the lighter 'sweet' crude have different applications dependent upon the capacity of each respective refinery. For example, sweet crude is preferred by refiners in the production of diesel fuel, jet fuel, gasoline and heating oil.

Gold

What is it?

Mined by the Egyptians over 4,000 years ago, gold has been coveted for centuries for its unique blend of beauty and rarity. The first gold coins date back to the 6th century BC, when they were produced upon the command of King Croesus of Lydia. It is a yellow, dense metallic element with a high lustre and is an inactive substance, unaffected by heat, air, moisture and most solvents. Because of this virtual indestructibility, all the gold that has ever been mined is still in circulation around the world in one form or another.

Who produces it?

It is mined on every continent except Antarctica, where mining is banned. South Africa is the largest producing nation, closely followed by the United States, Australia, China, Russia and Canada.

What is it used for?

Apart from the obvious cosmetic uses such as jewellery and decorative gold leaf, it is a vital industrial commodity, where its prime application is in electronics because of its excellent qualities as a conductor of heat and electricity. Another important industrial demand comes from dentistry, where gold has been used for nearly 3,000 years.

Heating oil

What is it?

Heating oil is a petroleum-based product that represents approximately a quarter of the refining output from a barrel of crude oil.

Who produces it?

The main consumer of heating oil, namely the United States, produces 85 per cent of its own requirement and imports the remainder from Canada, Venezuela and the Virgin Islands.

What is it used for?

As the name suggests, it is primarily used for providing fuel to heat properties.

Lead

What is it?

Lead was one of the first metals known to humankind. It is a dense, bluish-grey and highly toxic metallic element. Originally used in paints, plumbing and face powders and as a preservative in wine, many civilizations, including the Roman Empire, were unaware of its toxic effect, which resulted in vast numbers of their citizens being slowly poisoned by its use in everyday applications. Lead is usually found in ore with copper, silver and zinc but more than 50 per cent of the lead currently in use comes from recycling.

Who produces it?

China and the United States combined are responsible for nearly half of the world's lead smelter production, with Germany and the United Kingdom also smelting a notable percentage.

What is it used for?

Owing to its high density and nuclear properties, lead is used extensively in protective shielding for radioactive materials such as X-ray apparatus. It is also used in the construction industry and in the manufacture of electric cables and storage batteries.

Lean hogs (I do not participate in this market)

What are they?

'Hogs' is a US term for pigs. They are generally bred twice a year in a continuous cycle. The gestation period is three and a half months, producing an average litter of 9–10 piglets, and the time period from birth to slaughter is usually around six months.

Who produces them?

China is the largest producer of pork, followed by the European Union and then the United States. For the supply/demand argument of this book, as well as being the biggest producer of pork China is also the world's biggest consumer.

What are they used for?

The meat is primarily used as a food for humans. Following slaughter, an average carcass produces 85 pounds of lean meat, of which 21 per cent is ham, 20 per cent is loin, 14 per cent is belly and 3 per cent is spare ribs, with the remainder providing sundry carnivore products. The skin is often used to produce suede for clothing and footwear.

Live cattle (I do not participate in this market)

What are they?

Live cattle form part of the beef industry. Most ranchers manage their herds to produce new crops of calves every spring following a gestation period of nine months. Calves are weaned from their mothers after approximately six months and then spend the next 10 months foraging on summer grass or winter wheat until their weight reaches around 600 pounds. The cattle are then sent to a feedlot where they add a further 600 pounds and are ready for slaughter.

Who produces them?

The world's largest producer of beef is the United States, followed by Brazil, the European Union and China.

What are they used for?

The meat is primarily used as a food for humans and its consumption has recently enjoyed an increase following the popularity of high-protein diets such as the Atkins. The animal skin is used in the supply of leather for the manufacture of clothing and footwear.

Lumber

What is it?

Basically lumber is wood. It is produced from both hardwood, which comes from deciduous trees with broad leaves, and softwood, which comes from cone-bearing trees. Humankind has used wood for tools, building and energy since prehistoric times, and despite advances in the building and construction industry demand for this raw material remains as strong as ever.

Who produces it?

Wood is grown and utilized throughout the world, with the largest producers being the United States, Canada and Russia.

What is it used for?

Higher-quality wood is used for furniture, panelling, flooring and other decorative pieces whilst the lower grades are used for all manner of industrial applications, in particular home building.

Natural gas

What is it?

Natural gas is a colourless and odourless fossil fuel when in its natural form and is a mixture of many hydrocarbon gases including methane, propane and butane. Over 2,500 years ago, the Chinese harnessed the power of natural gas energy when they directed it through bamboo-shoot pipes and then burnt it to boil sea water to create fresh water.

Who produces it?

Russia and the United States are responsible for nearly two-thirds of the world's natural gas production, with Canada the other significant producer.

What is it used for?

Being a far cheaper source of energy than electricity, natural gas is widely used in residential properties for both heating and cooking. Large industry is also a major consumer for the same economic reasons.

Nickel

What is it?

Nickel is a hard, ductile metal and slightly silvery in appearance. It is found in all soil and also on the ocean floor and in meteorites. Its uses can be traced back as far as 3500 BC, when bronzes from what is now Syria had a nickel content. The Chinese also minted coins from this transition metal over 2,000 years ago. It is a good conductor of electricity and heat and is often combined with other metals, such as iron, copper, zinc and chromium, to form alloys.

Who produces it?

Russia, Australia, Canada and Indonesia are the world's largest miners of nickel.

What is it used for?

Nickel is primarily used in the production of corrosion-resistant alloys such as stainless steel. It is also employed as a replacement for silver in coins and in electronic circuitry, and nickel-plating techniques are utilized on rolled steel strip, helicopter rotor blades and turbine blades.

Orange juice

What is it?

Apart from drinking orange juice, the other exposure you may have had to this market is if you remember watching the hit film *Trading Places* starring Eddie Murphy, Dan Ackroyd and Jamie Lee Curtis where the final sequences heavily featured the orange juice futures pit in New York. The orange tree is semi-tropical and its fruit, the orange, is technically a kind of berry. There are three varieties of oranges: the sweet orange, the mandarin orange (also known as a tangerine) and the sour orange.

Who produces it?

Brazil is the largest producer, responsible for over a third of the world's oranges, with the United States and Mexico combining to produce another 30 per cent plus.

What is it used for?

Sweet oranges are primarily used for the production of orange juice, a healthy drink rich in vitamin C. Sour oranges are predominately used in the manufacture of marmalade and also as an ingredient in some liqueurs. Orange oil is a by-product obtained from the peel prior to juice extraction and is used in a variety of products from cleaning agents through to flavourings and perfumes.

Platinum

What is it?

Often referred to as 'the noble metal', it is one of the world's rarest commodities. To illustrate, if all the platinum ever mined in the world was collected together, it wouldn't fill an average-size living room. In addition to being limited in supply it is also extremely hard to produce, requiring the mining of between 8 and 10 tons of ore to produce just one pure ounce of platinum. It is a greyish-white, chemically inert metallic element that weighs almost twice as much as gold and has a greater value. It is also considered to be 'the metal of the future' because of its importance in various environmentally friendly applications.

Who produces it?

South Africa accounts for nearly 75 per cent of world supply with Russia, Canada and the United States the other principal producers.

What is it used for?

Platinum is highly prized by the jewellery industry, which accounts for just over half its consumption. The remaining demand comes from a variety of applications from fibre optic cables and infrared detectors through to anti-cancer drugs. However, the largest industrial use for platinum comes from the manufacture of automobile catalytic converters, devices fitted to vehicles and designed to convert harmful exhaust emissions such as oxides of nitrogen into water and other harmless substances.

Silver

What is it?

Mined in Asia Minor since before 2500 BC, silver was used by the ancient Greeks to produce the first silver coins around 700 BC and still today in many countries silver is used as a circulating coinage. Silver is a white, lustrous metallic element and is usually found combined with other elements in ores and minerals.

Who produces it?

In ancient times, silver was easy to find, with many deposits located on or near the earth's surface. Today, the majority of silver comes from Mexico, Peru, Australia, China and the United States where it is mined in conjunction with zinc, copper and lead.

What is it used for?

Because silver conducts heat and electricity better than any other metal, its primary application is as an industrial commodity. Photographic materials account for over half of its demand followed by conductors and contacts for the electronics industry. Surprisingly, only a small percentage, less than 3 per cent, is used for jewellery.

Soybean

What is it?

The soybean is a member of the oilseed family and is the common name for the leguminous plant and its seed. An ancient food in the Far East, it has a high protein content that has made it a popular food source throughout the world. The seeds are usually light yellow in colour, contained typically three to a pod with the plants themselves generally reaching maturity around 140 days after planting.

Who produces it?

The United States accounts for nearly 40 per cent of total world production with Brazil producing a further 20 per cent plus. Argentina is another major source of soybeans, closely followed by China, although as with most commodities nowadays China consumes considerably more soybeans than it produces.

What is it used for?

To produce a varied and diverse number of food products. Soy-based products are particularly popular with vegetarians because of their high non-meat protein content and also with consumers of non-dairy products such as soy milk, soy baby formula, soy cheese and soy nut butter.

Soybean meal

What is it?

Soybean meal is produced through the processing of soybeans, which are separated into both meal and soybean oil. This process is known in the industry as the 'soybean crush'. The conventional 'crush' model states that one bushel of soybeans, weighing approximately 60 pounds, will produce after processing: 11 pounds of oil, 44 pounds of minimum content protein meal, 3 pounds of hulls and 1 pound of waste. Meal represents about 35 per cent of the weight of raw soybeans, and processors aim to produce a conditioned product with a minimum protein content of 48 per cent, a minimum fat content of 0.5 per cent, a maximum moisture content of 12 per cent and a maximum fibre content of 3.5 per cent.

Who produces it?

The world's largest producers of soybean meal are the United States, which is responsible for 25 per cent of production, closely followed by Brazil, China and the European Union.

What is it used for?

The majority of soybean meal is used as a feed for poultry where it accounts for approximately two-thirds of the world's high-protein animal feed. The remaining meal is further processed to produce soy flour and isolated soy protein.

Soybean oil

What is it?

It is the natural oil extracted from whole soybeans as a result of the 'soybean crush' process. The conventional 'crush' model states that one bushel of soybeans, weighing approximately 60 pounds, will produce after processing: 11 pounds of oil, 44 pounds of minimum content protein meal, 3 pounds of hulls and 1 pound of waste. The oil content of each crop is directly correlated to the amount of sunshine and the temperatures during the soybean pod-filling stage. Typically, nearly 20 per cent of a soybean's weight can be extracted as oil.

Who produces it?

The United States accounts for over a quarter of world soybean oil production. Brazil is also a significant producer responsible for nearly 20 per cent, with the European Union accounting for a further 8 per cent.

What is it used for?

Being high in polyunsaturated fat and cholesterol free, soybean oil is used in a number of edible products from margarine to cooking and salad oils. It is also used in a number of inedible products such as resins, plastics, paints and varnishes.

Sugar

What is it?

Sugar is a carbohydrate compound. It is a white crystalline organic substance also known as sucrose. Whilst it is found in most plants, it occurs with the highest concentration in sugar beets and sugar cane. The former is grown in cooler climates whilst sugar cane prospers in the tropical regions between the Tropics of Cancer and Capricorn where it benefits from the warmer and more humid conditions. Although the sugar contained in both is identical, sugar beet is an annual grown from seed whilst sugar cane is a perennial plant grown from cuttings of the stalk and provides around 75 per cent of all sugar produced.

Who produces it?

Well over a hundred countries produce sugar, with Brazil currently the largest. Other major producers include the European Union and India.

What is it used for?

Primarily as a taste additive to foodstuffs and as a source of energy both for humans and in the composition of fuel derivatives such as ethanol.

Tin

What is it?

Tin is a soft and pliable metallic element with a high crystalline structure. Silver-white in appearance, it has been in use for over 5,000 years. During the Roman Empire, Cornwall was responsible for the majority of tin production and continued to be a leading source of the metal until the late 19th century. Nowadays, tin deposits are generally small and are often recovered as a by-product of mining lead and tungsten.

Who produces it?

Currently Indonesia is the largest miner of tin, responsible for over a third of world production. Not far behind is China, which produces nearly 25 per cent, and Peru, which accounts for a further 20 per cent. The world's largest producers of smelted tin are China, Indonesia and Malaysia. Although a large user of tin, the United States does not mine a single ounce of the metal and, apart from recycling scrap, it has to import the rest.

What is it used for?

Tin is primarily used in the manufacture of coatings for steel containers used to preserve food and beverages. It is also used in electroplating, plastic, ceramics and solder alloys. As tin is relatively low in toxicity, modern research is now focused on incorporating tin into a number of applications as a lead replacement.

Unleaded gasoline

What is it?

Gasoline is a mixture of hundreds of lighter liquid hydrocarbons and is primarily used to fuel the internal-combustion engine. It is a product refined from crude oil with refineries able to turn more than half of every barrel of crude into gasoline. The gasoline is then blended with ethanol (an alcohol-based product made from corn, wheat, barley and sugar), to produce a fuel with less harmful exhaust emissions.

Who produces it?

Refineries of varying size and capacity exist all over the world for the purpose of converting crude oil into gasoline and other petroleum-based products.

What is it used for?

Its primary use is as a fuel for the internal-combustion engine most commonly found in automobiles, articulated transporters and motor-cycles.

Wheat

What is it?

Originally a wild grass, wheat has been grown and cultivated by humans since prehistoric times. Now technically regarded as a cereal grass, it is responsible for supplying about 20 per cent of the food calories to the world's population.

Who produces it?

The European Union, thanks in part to heavy central government subsidies, is the world's largest producer of wheat, closely followed by China, India, Russia and the United States. Once again, for the supply/demand argument of this book, China, despite being the world's second-largest producer, actually consumes more wheat than it produces!

What is it used for?

Wheat is primarily used to produce flour but also has other applications including the making of oil, gluten, bedding, brewing and distilling alcohol and as a feed for livestock.

Zinc

What is it?

A bluish-white metallic element, zinc is never found in its pure state but rather as an oxide, sulphide, carbonate or silicate. It is also found in many minerals such as smithsonite, franklinite, sphalerite, hemimorphite and zincite. Zinc is used as an alloy with copper to make brass and also as an alloy with magnesium and aluminium.

Who produces it?

The world's largest producer of zinc is China, which is responsible for nearly 25 per cent of world smelter production. Canada, Japan and Australia are the other significant producers.

What is it used for?

It is used as a protective coating for other metals such as steel and iron. Zinc is also used in the manufacture of certain battery cells used in cameras, watches and other electronic equipment and, additionally, in medical applications primarily as an antiseptic.

The CRB Index (The Reuters/Jefferies CRB Futures Index)

The CRB Index offers commodity exposure in a similar way to how a stock market index provides exposure to a broad spectrum of capital weighted stocks and shares. It is calculated to produce a broad representation of the average overall trend in commodity markets, and the Commodity Research Bureau constantly monitors the component commodities to ensure the index provides as accurate a representation of price movements as possible. Following its ninth re-weighting in July 2005, the Reuters/Jefferies CRB Index currently comprises the following 19 commodities:

aluminium	
cocoa	live cattle
coffee	natural gas
copper	nickel
corn	orange juice
cotton	silver
crude oil	soybeans
gold	sugar
heating oil	unleaded gas
lean hogs	wheat

The CRB Index began life in 1957 and is now recognized as the main barometer of overall commodity trends. It serves as an excellent price measure for macroeconomic analysis. It provides an efficient and cost-effective option for those seeking to gain a simple exposure to commodities as an asset class. The only potential drawback is a fixed minimum weighting of 33 per cent for the energy sector. Whilst this is a lower weighting than the Goldman Sachs Index discussed later, such a weighting can make the CRB more of an energy proxy than was previously the case. However, it is still a viable alternative for those investors who have neither the time nor the expertise to deal with individual commodities.

The DJ–AIGCI (The Dow Jones-AIG Commodity Index)

The components of the Dow Jones–AIG Index are annually re-weighted based upon the procedures set forth in the *DJ–AIGCI Handbook*, which states the composition of the index is 'dependent on a combination of factors related to liquidity and US dollar-weighted production data over the most recently available five years'. It attempts, as all the other commodity indices attempt as well, to represent as accurately as possible the importance of a diversified group of commodities and their economic significance. The Dow Jones–AIG Commodity Index currently comprises the following 20 commodities:

aluminium	live cattle
cocoa	natural gas
coffee	nickel
copper	silver
corn	soybeans
cotton	soybean oil
crude oil	sugar
gold	unleaded gas
heating oil	wheat
lean hogs	zinc

Despite the differences in its method of weighting, this index also carries a heavy energy sector component, with the combined energy commodities representing more than a third of its total performance. However, it is still a viable alternative for those investors who have neither the time nor the expertise to deal with the individual commodity markets.

The GSCI (The Goldman Sachs Commodity Index)

The components of the Goldman Sachs Index are weighted based upon the world production figures of each respective commodity. They state that 'the quantity of each commodity in the index is determined by the average quantity of production in the last five years'. Goldman Sachs feel it's better to construct their index in this way because it assigns the correct weighting in relation to the proportion of the amount that each commodity flows through the economy. Using this method to determine the composition of the index generally means a stronger weighting towards the energy sector and, as at 30 June 2005, the current weightings detailed on the Goldman Sachs Commodity Index website show that the energy sector is responsible for a massive 75 per cent of the performance of the entire index. This can be a double-edged sword because, if the energy commodities have a strong performance, as is currently the case, this index will perform better than any other commodity proxy. However, should the energy sector underperform, then an investment in the Goldman Sachs Index will lag behind a similar investment in the other commodity-based indices. The Goldman Sachs Commodity Index currently comprises the following 24 commodities:

aluminium	lead
Brent crude oil	lean hogs
cocoa	live cattle
coffee	natural gas
copper	nickel
corn	red wheat
cotton	silver
crude oil	soybeans
feeder cattle	sugar
gas oil	unleaded gas
gold	wheat
heating oil	zinc

Similarly to the other commodity indices, the Goldman Sachs Commodity Index provides an efficient and cost-effective option for those seeking to gain a simple exposure to commodities as an asset class. The only reservation I have with the GSCI is its over-concentration of exposure to the energy sector, which makes this index more of an energy proxy than a commodity proxy. However, it can still be a viable alternative for those investors who do not wish to deal with the individual commodity markets.

Commodity investment options

An important aspect we need to cover is which instrument or investment vehicle you will use to participate in this commodity bull market. For those readers domiciled in the United Kingdom, I suggest you consider establishing all your investment positions as spread bets.

Tax-free investing

Spread betting offers the exciting opportunity to participate in and profit from this investment boom without having to pay any capital gains tax (applicable to UK residents – investors from other countries need to conduct their own due diligence). Yes, if you establish and maintain your commodity investments via spread betting, all your profits will be tax free and, not only that, this type of investing is regulated by the Financial Services Authority (the UK financial services regulator).

Spread betting in the UK has been around for over 20 years. Initially aimed at and used by dealers in the City of London, spread betting is now growing in popularity throughout the country. As I mentioned earlier, its main benefit is that, under current UK legislation (which could always change in the future), investment profits are not subject to capital gains tax. To illustrate just how powerful this tax-free status is to your investment returns, let's look at the following example. We have two hypothetical investments of £50,000 each. Both investments are identical in every way except investment A pays a capital gains tax of 40 per cent on all annual profits whilst investment B is allowed to compound all annual profits as it doesn't pay any tax. Assuming a 10-year performance where each year saw both investments gross a 10 per cent annual return, investment A would have grown to £89,542 (a gain of 79 per cent) whilst investment B would have grown to £129,687 (a gain of 159 per cent). Where else can you double the performance of an investment without any additional risk?

Another advantage to spread betting is the ability to establish a credit account. Subject to satisfying the spread-betting firm you have the necessary money, using a credit account means you can hold a spread-betting position whilst still retaining your investment cash in an interest-bearing bank or building society account. Should the commodity investment prove immediately profitable, you could find yourself in the comfortable position of earning interest on your investment cash whilst also building up profits from the commodity markets. However, if your market position begins to show a loss, you will be required to cover the deficit with a transfer of cash to the credit account.

How spread betting works

Spread betting has a wide range of applications suitable for a broad spectrum of investors, enabling them to 'bet' on the price movements of numerous shares, stock indices, bonds, currencies and commodity futures. Typically, the larger spread-betting firms will quote on all the major markets 24 hours a day between Sunday night and the close of business in the United States on a Friday night. When you make a spread bet, you never actually own the stock, bond or commodity. Instead you 'buy' the spread-betting broker's quote when you bet that a market will rise. If the market subsequently goes up as you predicted, your winnings multiply. Conversely, if the market moves in the opposite direction to your prediction, then your losses will multiply. Similarly to using futures, it is also possible with spread betting to control a large amount of money with a small cash deposit and, whilst this leverage sounds exciting, I want firmly to dissuade any novice from investing in this fashion. If you still do not fully understand the subject of leverage, please refer back to Chapter 4.

A spread is a quote made up of two prices, which straddle the underlying market price. The higher 'offer' price is for buyers and the lower 'bid' price is for sellers. Let's look at an example of investing in silver. The commodity has a futures contract and the price quoted by the spread-betting broker will be based upon the market price of this futures contract. It's July, and your strategy indicates that you should invest in this commodity. You call your spread-betting broker for a price of the September contract (the nearest and most active futures contract is usually known as the 'front month') and the quote is 725–729. You buy £10 a point at 729. This is the equivalent of approximately a £7,300 investment in silver (£10 multiplied by the spread-bet purchase price of 729 = £7,290). Let's suppose your position turns out to be correct and a few weeks later your strategy instructs you to close your position for a profit. The spread-betting broker is now quoting 838–842 for the September contract and you close your position by selling the spread £10 a point at 838. You have now made a profit of 838 − 729 = 109 points. At £10 a point this represents a £1,090 profit (109 × £10), and a 15 per cent gain in the value of the commodity has produced a tax-free return of around 15 per cent on your £7,300 original investment.

If your strategy hasn't provided an exit signal and the futures contract in which you hold your position reaches its expiry, you will have to 'roll over' your position as this 'front month' contract matures. 'Roll-over' is simply market terminology for moving your position from one contract to another. This is not as complicated as it sounds, because the spread-betting broker usually advises by letter when a contract is approaching its expiry date. When they write, they will ask if you wish to close the position upon expiry or 'roll' the position to the next contract. Unless you wish to close or readjust the size of your position, all you need to do is call them and confirm that you wish the position to be 'rolled over'. Typically, for this type of instruction, the spread-betting firm charges only a minimal spread (fee). It's important to be aware that, as this commodity boom could run for many years, you may need to keep rolling your spread-betting position forward as each futures contract expires until such time as you 'cash in your chips' and close your investment. To close a position, simply sell whichever contract month your position is currently held in.

If you ever need help in identifying the current front month or in calculating the size of your spread bet relative to your financial commitment, the broker will always be able to help, and you should never feel uncomfortable about asking even the most basic of questions. It's better to be safe than sorry.

Getting started in spread betting

To begin spread betting, you first need to open an account with a regulated spread-betting broker. The Financial Services Authority (details in Appendix A) will be able to provide a list of all the regulated spread-betting firms. You should contact a number of these to obtain the most competitive bid–offer spread rates, and once you have found a suitable candidate you are ready to open an account. Typically, a spread-betting account involves the extension of credit to the client via a review of their personal finances and proof of liquid assets (cash). All this is normally covered in the formal account-opening documentation, but this can take a couple of weeks to process, so if you want to set up your account more quickly you should consider opening a deposit account instead. A deposit account is slightly different in that you are required to 'deposit' cash with the spread-betting broker before you can begin investing.

In addition, spread-betting brokers can provide you with detailed regulatory approved literature that further explains the mechanics and process of spread betting, and some even conduct free seminars to help new participants gain a greater understanding. If you are new to the business, I recommend you take full advantage of all the helpful information these brokers provide. After all, it's in their interest to see you succeed, as the more money you make the more you will use them and the greater their commission revenue will become. Nobody benefits if a new customer loses money and then quits.

Another investment option – the futures contract

As I've just reviewed, spread-betting brokers use an underlying futures contract on which to base their quotes, so for the benefit of those new to spread betting and for the non-UK-domiciled investors who gain no tax benefit from spread betting I want briefly to provide a little more information about the futures contract itself.

The idea of using futures is not new. This notion of fixing a price now and settling later can be traced back to 2000 BC when the merchants of Bahrain took goods on consignment for barter in India. A rudimentary form of the risk-eliminating futures contract originated in England in the 18th century, whereby two parties would agree in advance to the terms of a sale, which was not finalized until the goods arrived. Such contracts of sale on a 'to arrive' basis were made as early as 1780 in the Liverpool cotton trade. Commodity exchanges originated in the latter part of the 19th century as a means whereby merchants could rely on a guaranteed price for goods they had to ship over great distances. In this way, they could avoid the risk of price fluctuations eradicating their profits during the long, slow shipment. The sale price was fixed at the time of shipment and a deposit paid but the goods themselves were not delivered until a future date, at which time the balance of the purchase price became payable. In 1884, an organized futures market with rules and regulations was founded in Chicago, Illinois. The Chicago Board of Trade was to go on to fashion and operate the first futures contract in a form that the English grain markets were to copy over 30 years later. In the mid-1970s a revolution began to take place in the futures markets with the introduction of financial futures. The main Chicago exchanges, looking at the behaviour of some financial securities such as shares and bonds, which were bought and sold around the world, realized that many of them behaved in much the same way as commodity markets. There appeared to be a need to provide the financial world with an opportunity to hedge and speculate against the underlying cash markets and so the financial futures contract was born. Warning – futures contracts enable participants to leverage their cash aggressively and it is for this reason that I caution you to understand fully the subject of leverage, which was discussed earlier in the book, before using them.

How futures contracts work

Basically, a futures contract is an agreement between two parties (a buyer and seller) for settlement of a specified security or commodity at a certain price on a given future date, as established on the floor of an authorized futures exchange. It is a legal contract and in certain cases can be fulfilled by the delivery and acceptance of the physical commodity. However, the existence of clearing houses makes each contract transferable and most futures contracts are closed out with an offsetting futures transaction. To facilitate the clearing process, futures contracts on the organized exchanges are standardized with regard to the quantity and specific characteristics of the relevant underlying commodity or financial security. In all cases, the relevant market authority determines the minimum tradable quantity; the prescribed minimum is called a 'lot' or 'contract'. Lot sizes are published for each futures market. The variables are the price, the delivery date, the contract month and the identity of the buyer and seller. Most futures contracts start one year before their maturity but some have lives as long as three years or more.

A futures contract is quoted in two prices. The higher 'offer' price is for buyers and the lower 'bid' price is for sellers. The process of using a futures contract to invest, including both 'front month' and 'roll-over' procedures, is identical to spread betting, the only difference being that the bid and offer spread prices will be smaller. This is because you pay a commission to the futures broker whenever you trade, whereas the spread-betting firm include any costs in the spread itself, which makes their bid–offer price difference larger. In addition, because futures contracts have a fixed value with specified minimum price movements, they are slightly less flexible than spread betting.

Getting started in futures

To begin using futures contracts, you first need to open an account with a regulated futures broker. The Financial Services Authority (details in Appendix A) will be able to provide a list of all the regulated futures brokerage firms. You should contact a number of these to obtain the most competitive commission rates and, once you have found a suitable candidate, you are ready to open an account. Typically, a futures account operates in exactly the same way as a spread-betting deposit account where you are required to 'deposit' cash with the broker before you can begin investing.

In addition, some futures brokers will provide you with detailed regulatory approved literature that further explains the mechanics and processes of using futures contracts. If you are new to the business, I recommend you take full advantage of all the helpful information these brokers provide. After all, it's in their interest to see you succeed, as the more money you make the more you will use them and the greater their commission revenue will become. Just as with spread betting, nobody benefits if a new customer loses money and then quits.

Another investment option – commodity-based funds

Although I rarely invest in mutual funds, there are a couple on the radar offering general exposure to commodities. In addition, there are numerous other funds available that primarily concentrate on the energy and/or metals sectors. Those investors who wish to participate in the boom but do not want to use spread betting or futures contracts should consider using these funds as an alternative. I have included these two funds for your information only and strongly recommend you consult an independent financial adviser (IFA) to obtain recent and past performance data and discuss fees, bid–offer spreads, minimum subscription terms, redemption periods and other related items before investing.

- *Oppenheimer Real Asset Fund.* This is an actively managed product managed by a large and well-respected company. As with most commodity proxies, it is heavily weighted towards the energy sector with more than a 70 per cent exposure according to an article in *Forbes* (June 2005).
- *Pimco Commodity Real Return Fund.* This product is the larger of the two, based upon assets under management, and is designed passively to track the performance of the Dow Jones–AIG Commodity Index. It primarily achieves this goal through using futures contracts based upon the DJ–AIGCI.

I'm sure as the commodity boom unfolds there will be plenty more commodity-based funds on offer as institutions attempt to cash in on the rally. The fact that there aren't that many funds around at the moment is further confirmation that this boom is still in its early stages and when an exponential increase in the number of these products does occur it will help us identify that the trend has entered its final stage.

Another investment option – commodity stocks and shares

Another way to play this commodity boom is to identify and monitor listed companies whose business activity is primarily commodity based. Mining and oil exploration companies have been in the headlines recently and I'm sure there is plenty of potential for these and other similar stocks. My only reservation about investing in individual stocks and shares over and above the commodity markets themselves is that individual companies are susceptible to additional performance risks such as industrial action, taxation and general mismanagement.

Which investment option you decide to use is, of course, your decision. Personally, I direct all my long-term investing through the tax-efficient route of spread betting, but all of the options I've discussed here are viable ways to participate in a commodity bull market.

Conclusion

Of all the bankers, brokers, analysts, investment advisers, fund managers, market commentators and investors, not many involved in the markets today have lived through, let alone participated in, a boom in commodities. Therefore, they have no first-hand knowledge of such a trend. In fact, recent experiences from the last two decades will have left them with the impression that, at best, 'commodities always flatter to deceive'. Well, nothing lasts for ever and the same is true of the commodity markets – the game has now changed and we have re-entered a period of profit opportunity not seen since the late 1960s. In fact, there are a number of parallels that can be drawn between then and now, namely: commodity prices are at historically low levels, forcing producers to run down inventories rather than increase production; there is excessive credit creation flooding the system with liquidity; there is a weakening US dollar; and, finally, there is US participation in expensive and ultimately drawn-out overseas military operations. Those who point to the recent gains in commodity prices over the last two years as a 'bubble' fail to recognize that this rally has been from historically low levels and, on an inflation-adjusted basis, prices still need to rally over 175 per cent just to reach their supply-disrupted peak of 1980.

Over the next few years, the demand from approximately 2.6 billion new consumers, nearly half of the world's entire population, is going to put a tremendous strain upon commodity suppliers and, in many cases, the natural resources just aren't there to meet this demand. This will, in turn, create massive supply/demand imbalances and powerful market trends. Such profitable investment trends don't come along that often, and opportunities to make triple-digit returns in a short space of time occur with even less frequency. This commodity boom will be one that lasts for at least another 10 years, and although it won't be without its fair share of shocks and scares along the way it offers the opportunity for those with foresight to achieve tremendous percentage returns – profits that could make all other recent bull markets and investment bubbles seem tame by comparison.

The commodity markets are already moving up and will continue to do so for longer and further than most 'experts' predict. These high prices will affect every one of us, and ignoring this trend could be costly, as it will eventually trigger the return of higher inflation. High inflation reduces your ability to maintain your current standard of living; it increases the real cost of both essential and luxury purchases; and it erodes the value of the cash in your pocket and bank account. High inflation will eventually result in higher interest rates, and any outstanding debts, be they credit cards, hire purchase agreements, personal loans or mortgages on residential and/or investment properties, will become more expensive to administer.

To mitigate the negative effects of such a commodity boom, you need to profit from it. Not only does this book alert you to this fantastic investment opportunity, but it also provides you with tried-and-tested strategies to help you participate – strategies that I am using myself at this very moment. What you decide to do is of course up to you. Long-term trend following is not rocket science and, if you can adopt the correct psychological mindset and remain sufficiently capitalized, it does work.

Thank you for your time, and remember, 'Luck rewards the prepared.'

Appendix A – Useful contacts

United Kingdom

Financial Services Authority (FSA)
25 The Colonnade
Canary Wharf
London E14 5HS
Consumer help line: 0845 606 1234

Financial Ombudsman Service
South Quay Plaza
183 Marsh Wall
London E14 9SR
Consumer help line: 0845 080 1800
www.financial-ombudsman.org.uk

United States of America

Commodity Futures Trading Commission (CFTC)
Three Lafayette Center
1155 21st Street, NW
Washington, DC 20581
Complaint line: 866-FON-CFTC or 202 418 5000

www.cftc.gov

Securities and Exchange Commission (SEC)
Complaint Center
100F Street, NE
Washington, DC 20549-0213
Tel: 1-800-SEC-0330 or 202 942 8088
www.sec.gov

Appendix B –
An interview with
Mark Shipman

This interview was conducted on 5 August 2004 and appears on the www.trend-follower.com website. It is reproduced here for information purposes only.

How did you get into the business?
I began in the 1980s, when I had an opportunity to change my career path from accountancy to working in the dealing room of the French bank I was with at the time.

What made you change?
Boredom! I had been working in the accounts departments of various banks for over seven years and was literally one step away from becoming a branch accountant but I hated what I was doing. The dealers at the bank seemed to be having a lot more fun and getting better paid for it.

How long did it take before you were profitable?
I made a profit from my first ever position, although I soon realized that was down to pure luck rather than good judgement. It actually took a couple of years to really establish myself. I must have read every book on investing in addition to spending many hours at work and at home testing strategies by hand using hundreds of price charts and a large magnifying glass!

Why did you elect to conduct your research by hand? Do you think computer-based research is defective?

Unfortunately, at the time, the affordable personal computer hadn't been invented so I was forced to conduct all my research using books of historical price charts. Nowadays, things are a lot easier with relatively inexpensive and very powerful computers in addition to some excellent off-the-shelf programming software and cheap but accurate historical data. If all this had been easily available over 20 years ago, I would have quite happily abandoned the magnifying glass.

Are there any negatives to computer-based research?

Computers are just tools for leveraging research. They provide tremendous analytical power but in the wrong hands they can also produce very misleading information. They're great at getting large technical research tasks completed quickly, nothing more.

So what are their pitfalls?

When using a computer to research historical price data there is always a risk that it will just identify the most profitable strategies. This might sound like what a computer should be doing but you're 'data mining' and treading on very dangerous ground. Researchers must remember that the goal for testing is to develop robust, logical and practical strategies and they must be careful not to abuse the powerful research capabilities of a computer. Anyone with the benefit of hindsight can research and develop a strategy with a fantastic past record but the real money is only made if it works in the future. Fortunately, there are some safeguards that can be taken to counter this 'over-optimization'.

Can you share them?

Firstly, I only research the performance of a new strategy up to a specific point in history, say starting 15 years ago up to five years ago. Then, if the results are satisfactory I test the strategy on the last five years up to the present day. This 'forward-looking' research assumes that, if a strategy has been over-optimized up to my cut-off point five years ago, then it should be exposed in the next five years' worth of data. If the performance remains consistent, then the first hurdle has been cleared. My second guideline is what I call my 'commonsense test'. Forgetting how historically profitable the strategy I've developed might actually be, I always question whether its rules make sense from a market viewpoint and, also, that they are compatible with how I prefer to operate. If not, sooner or later I will abandon the strategy because I'm uncomfortable with the signals it's providing. One final protection from over-optimizing is the number of rules the strategy contains. The fewer the number of rules, the more robust it is.

Now would seem a good time to ask you to describe your method of operation?
Because I'm a long-term investor, I'm looking for the big macro trends and, although I use some fundamental analysis to identify a potential asset class, the most important factor in my investing is 'timing' and for that I focus on technical analysis, primarily using weekly bar charts with an emphasis on breakouts and reversal patterns. Whatever the fundamentals may indicate, I find price charts are extremely helpful in gauging market sentiment and I always give greater preference to my chart-based analysis over any other input.

I usually conduct my investment analysis just once a week, normally at the weekend when the markets are closed. Typically the analysis takes no more than an hour in total but this streamlining is the result of many years of research and experience. Personally speaking, I think it's the quality of your analysis that produces the profitable investments rather than the quantity. On occasions, the markets have had nothing to offer my style of investing and I've spent many months and sometimes years without a position. For me, investing is all about long-term capital gains.

Do you use any of the popular technical indicators?
For trend following, I predominantly use weekly breakouts. For counter-trend price action, I use other pattern recognition algorithms. With regard to indicators such as RSIs, stochastics or guru-type analysis such as Gann or Elliott Wave, I personally have found little of value. The only use they may have is in providing the user with a discipline or plan.

What do you mean?
To give you an example, many years ago I met a fellow investor at a monthly meeting of the Society of Technical Analysts. We were discussing methods of investing and he announced he was an 'astro-analyst'! All his investments in the stock market were based upon where the

planets were in relationship to each other. He said if the market made a new high and Saturn was in line with Jupiter he would buy the market. Now, I like to maintain an open mind about most things but I was struggling to accept this type of analysis so I questioned him further. I asked what if the planets were in their correct places and he bought the market and it went down? He said he would close the position as the market was out of tune with the astral alignment. I then asked how he would react if he bought the market and it actually went up? He said he would run the position until the planets moved out of their alignment or the price dropped, which may take many weeks or months.

Now I got it. By using this unusual and highly questionable form of analysis in the fashion he was, my new acquaintance had simply found another way of imposing one of the most important rules of investing. He had a method for running his profits and cutting his losses. I think it had very little to do with Jupiter or Saturn. I believe it was his discipline that was making him the money.

Do you think discipline is that important?
I think discipline is one of the most important attributes an investor can have. If I don't possess the discipline to stick to my strategies, they mean nothing.

What other attributes do you consider essential?
Patience is another key ingredient. Investing is for the most part extremely testing psychologically because the markets don't always reward us for doing the right thing. This 'random reinforcement' can be both frustrating and destabilizing. The successful participant is one who has the discipline to remain true to his or her strategies and also possesses the patience to wait for the markets to behave in a more conducive fashion. Whatever your method of analysis is, participating in the markets is essentially a 'mind game' and controlling your emotions is ultimately the key to success. EQ (emotional intelligence) is far more important than IQ (intellectual intelligence) in investing. The psychological side of investing is the least understood and most often overlooked aspect of the business. Yet it's the most important.

Is it true you have studied hypnosis and neuro-linguistic programming?
Yes, I studied with Paul McKenna, the TV hypnotist. I find the psychological side of investing fascinating. It's similar to poker – the successful

players are the ones who know themselves, they know their own strengths and weaknesses and they are able to control their emotions and stick to their game plan whatever the circumstances or pressure.

What made you decide to teach others your methods and philosophy?
Well, I'm not going to give you the baloney some do about 'wanting to share their good fortune with others'. For me, I see the education and training products I'm associated with as another way of leveraging my expertise. If people like what I'm doing and want to learn more, then I'm happy to teach them. Another by-product of teaching is that it forces me to constantly research and re-evaluate my subject, which is no bad thing.

Also, without naming names, there are some so-called 'successful experts' teaching 'their' methods and charging innocent people large sums of money, when in actual fact these 'experts' either don't invest, can't invest or their profits are less than impressive. I thought, if they can do it, then why shouldn't I, because at least I'm the genuine article; at least I'm a successful investor.

Is being a successful investor really a skill you can learn?
Yes, of course it is. That's how I did it and I've already proved it by teaching others. It started when I spent some time with a friend of a friend. The guy was a former futures pit trader and, when the London futures exchange (LIFFE) closed its open outcry pits, he wanted to continue but was having trouble adjusting to operating away from the exchange floor. So, as a favour, I taught him my philosophies and some of my investment strategies.

Did he adapt to your methods?
It took him a little while to adapt to long-term investing, but once he did he became very successful.

To be taught your methods, do you think it's a prerequisite to have had some prior experience?
No, definitely not. In fact, I prefer to teach people who've had no previous experience. They're more like a blank canvas and don't have too many preconceived ideas. Novices are usually better at accepting new ideas, whereas people with prior 'market knowledge' often deviate when they think they know better.

Does that annoy you?
Not really. If they pay me to show them a strategy that's been hugely successful over many years and they ignore it, that's their choice.

Is it possible to operate your methods on a part-time basis?
Of course. In fact there isn't enough work required to make it a full-time activity. The amount of time required to conduct my investment analysis is usually only an hour a week in total. My methods are designed to identify and participate in long-term investment trends and as such require no input on a daily basis. In addition, as well as demanding less time than other methods, they are also infinitely cheaper to operate because the required market price information can be obtained from 'free-access' internet websites.

Do you think a system can outperform other forms of analysis?
Whether a systematic approach can outperform discretionary analysis really depends upon who is conducting the analysis. An exceptional investor would be hard to beat. However, such an individual only accounts for a tiny percentage of market participants, so I think, yes, a well-researched system could outperform the majority of investors in the long run. A systematic type of approach is definitely better for the novice if it imposes patience and discipline and forces users to cut their losses and run their profits. In a nutshell, following any sound investment strategy that guarantees the operator will be long in bull markets and neutral in bear markets is going to provide healthy, above-average investment returns.

Does a losing streak alter your approach?
It has no effect on my market analysis but, from a money management point of view, I might adjust the size of a new position if the level of my investment capital has been significantly reduced.

How do you handle the emotional effect of a losing streak?
Over the years I've had plenty of tough periods but I've never let them get to me. Years ago, I learnt a great psychological trick – keep things 'in perspective'. I'd say to myself, 'All right, I'm losing money, but no one is dead; no one is dying; no one is ill; it's just money.' That might sound a bit melodramatic, but would you swap the health of a loved one for a winning investment? Of course not, and that I think is the

key. Keeping a sense of perspective is also important in handling the winning streaks as well.

How so? Surely winning streaks don't cause problems?
Wrong. In fact, I think a winning streak can often be more destabilizing. Too much success can make people cocky, and some idiots believe they are so 'in tune' with the markets they can do no wrong. When this happens, they're in trouble because this overconfidence usually means they will ignore or abandon their original strategy because they now think they know better. When that happens, it's only a question of time before the market turns on them and they are wiped out!

If you can keep a sense of perspective through any winning period and rationalize that it might just be a lucky streak, then hopefully you won't get complacent. Also, too much elation during the good times and too much depression during the bad will eventually lead to emotional burn-out.

Do you set price targets?
I never set profit or price targets and all my analysis and position management is reactionary to recent market movements. I think price targets are pure guesswork and anyone who uses them runs the risk of exiting a great position too soon just because they have made a small gain.

Do you use stops?
Sometimes, although if anything was more of an art than a science it's the placing of stops. Retrospectively they are always either too tight or too far away, depending upon how the market has behaved. Often if a market has been in a strong trend, I will use a trailing stop but even then trailing stops are usually too far away and can often result in many a trend-following position sacrificing a large part of its unrealized profit. To counter this, I have developed a number of pattern recognition strategies that will jump in and close the longer-term position if the market behaves in a certain way. They are very good at protecting large amounts of unrealized profit.

What type of price action does your pattern recognition analysis focus on?
The patterns are variations of upside price failures and sharp reactions in bull trends.

What markets do you participate in?
Stock indices, individual shares, interest rate products, government bonds, rental property, commercial property, currencies and all the main commodities such as gold, silver, crude oil, coffee, wheat, soybeans, sugar, cocoa, etc, etc.

Do you attempt to hold a minimum number of positions in various different markets to maintain diversification?
No, all the positions I hold will be the result of good technical market action.

Do you ever conduct correlation analysis between the positions you hold and if so how?
No. Actually I think the 'diversification – low correlation' mantra is not conducive to maximizing profits. If a market is going up big-time, I want to be invested and likewise, if another market is going up, I want to be invested in that as well. I don't worry about how my positions look on a correlation basis; I just want to be invested in what's going up. To me that's logical.

You seem to have a knack for identifying big investment trends before they become common knowledge. Is there anything you're currently looking at?
Yes, most definitely. Commodities. I think we are at the beginning of a major bull market in commodity values and I'm investing accordingly.

Are your reasons fundamental or technical?
Both. Fundamentally, commodities are at their lowest levels since the Great Depression of the 1930s and this has led to a depletion in inventories coupled with an under-investment in production. Add to this a massive increase in demand from Asia for all things commodity and you have the potential for a tremendous bull market. Technically, many commodity markets are already beginning to exhibit the upward momentum I require to get my juices going. In fact, I feel more confident about this boom than I did about the property rental market back in 1994.

Aren't commodities just going to be another investment 'bubble'?
I hope so. 'Bubbles' are great ways to make money if you participate at the right time and don't outstay your welcome.

But how do you know when the trend is over?
Technically, the charts play an important role in alerting the savvy that the days of 'milk and honey' are finished. Another good indicator will be when my postman or the guy who reads my gas meter starts telling me they are speculating in commodities. When everybody thinks they're an expert, that's always a sign we're near the end.

Just how high do you see prices going?
As I've said before, price targets are pure guesswork but, if this bull market in commodities is stronger than the last one in the 1970s, and I suspect it will be, then I wouldn't be surprised to see crude oil over $100, gold over $1,000 and many others up tenfold.

Are there any other investors whom you respect?
I respect anyone who is prepared to risk their own money backing their own judgement. If they're successful, I respect them even more. For pure analytical skill, I'm a big fan of David Fuller and his 'behavioural' approach to the markets.

Finally, what advice would you give to a novice investor?
Don't rush in, take things slowly and obtain as much information on the subject as possible. Also, remain humble. I might appear confident in my ability as an investor but when it comes to participating in the markets I still remain humble. Always remember, the market is never wrong – but your position could be!

Appendix C – Sources for investment analysis

I conduct all my investment analysis using the internet. Utilizing free-access online charting websites, highly respected investment newsletters and off-the-shelf research software into which I can import data, I have found that all the information required to operate my strategies is just a few mouse clicks away.

Charting websites

www.barchart.com
A free-access website. Its 'Custom Chart' section enables users to program both weekly charts and moving averages. It offers comprehensive coverage of all the main commodity and financial futures markets and a select group of mutual funds as well.

www.bigcharts.com
A free-access website. Its 'Interactive Charting' section enables users to program both weekly charts and moving averages. It concentrates on global stocks and stock market indices.

www.futuresource.com
A free-access website. Its 'Studies/Indicators' section enables users to program both weekly charts and moving averages. It offers coverage of the main commodity and financial futures markets.

www.tradingcharts.com
A free-access website. Currently it only offers pre-set moving average indicators programmed into its charts and therefore is only of use to those investors who will be concentrating on the weekly breakout strategies.

Charting software programs

www.equis.com
Home page for the Metastock charting software product. The majority of the charts detailed in this book were produced using this program.

www.omnitrader.com
Home page for the Omnitrader charting software product.

www.paritech.co.uk
A distributor of chart analysis software programs and information downloading systems. If you wish to conduct your own historical research, this company is an excellent source of product. In particular, it acts as agent for both Metastock and Omnitrader, two highly sophisticated yet easy-to-operate software programs.

Investment research (newsletter) websites

www.dowtheoryletters.com
A long-standing subscription-based investment newsletter service written by the respected market commentator Richard Russell.

www.fullermoney.com
Offers a subscription-based global investment analysis service complete with a chart library. Written by one of my market heroes, David Fuller, this website also has a free-access section, which provides brief daily analysis of current market movements.

www.gloomboomdoom.com
Offers an excellent subscription-based monthly investment newsletter

produced by the highly respected market commentator Dr Marc Faber.

www.trend-follower.com
A free-access website, where I regularly post an investment diary detailing both my current long-term market analysis and investment positions.

Glossary of financial terms

Here is a brief glossary of financial and market terminology that may or may not be familiar to you. Most of the terms appear in this book at some point or other and the remainder I have included to be helpful.

analysts   Individuals who work for financial institutions such as banks and brokerage houses. Their job is to analyse and report upon various aspects of an investment and offer their opinion regarding its future profitability.
asset   Anything that is of any value to anyone, for example stocks and shares, property, bonds, vintage cars, antiques, etc.

bear   Someone who believes that market prices will fall.
bear market   A market where prices are falling.
bid–offer spread   The difference between the prices at which investors can buy and sell. The 'bid' is always the lower price and the 'offer' is always the higher price. The bigger the difference between the bid and the offer prices, the more expensive it is to participate.
bid price   The price at which investors can sell.
bull   Someone who believes that market prices will rise.
bull market   A market where prices are rising.

commodity futures contract   An agreement between two parties (a buyer and a seller) for delivery of a specified commodity on a given date in the future, as established on the platform of an authorized futures exchange.

CPI The Consumer Price Index provides a numerical representation of the changes in the prices paid by urban consumers for a basket of goods and services. As an economic indicator, it is the most widely used measure of inflation.

credit account A spread-betting account that allows the client, subject to numerous credit checks, to establish a position without first having to deposit cash with the spread-betting company.

deposit account A spread-betting account that requires the client to 'deposit' cash with the spread-betting company before any positions can be established.

Financial Ombudsman A body that acts as an arbitrator in complaints and disputes between financial companies and individuals.

Financial Services Authority (FSA) A government body empowered under the Financial Services Act to regulate the financial services industry.

front month Market terminology used to describe the most actively traded futures contract. The contract with the greatest liquidity.

investment capital An amount of money that can be invested free from the demands of daily, weekly, monthly or annual living expenses.

leverage The ability to control an amount of money greater than the amount of cash employed.

liquidity Terminology for any market where there are numerous buyers and sellers competing, thus making it easier to establish or close a position near the current market price.

long position A market position held to profit from a bull market in prices.

long-term My interpretation is any time period greater than a calendar week.

margin call A request made by a spread-betting broker to a client to deposit cash immediately to cover some or all of the client's exposure to loss.

offer price   The price at which investors can buy.

OPEC   Established in 1960, the Organization of Petroleum Exporting Countries has 11 members: Algeria, Indonesia, Iran, Iraq, Kuwait, Libya, Nigeria, Qatar, Saudi Arabia, United Arab Emirates and Venezuela.

risk   In the context of this book, the amount or the probability of an investment losing money.

Sharpe ratio   A measurement of performance developed by William F Sharpe. It is generally calculated as the rate of return minus a risk-free rate of return divided by the standard deviation for the period. In theory, the more positive the Sharpe ratio figure is, the better the performance.

short position   A market position held to profit from a bear market in prices.

short-term   My interpretation is any time period less than a calendar week.

spread betting   A tax-efficient, flexible medium for investing in the commodity markets.

technical analysis   The study of market price action through the use of charts.

trend   The sustained movement of market prices in a given direction (up or down).

Further reading

I credit a great deal of my personal success in the markets and in other areas of my investment career to the books I have read. In fact, almost all the information needed to succeed financially is readily available in books. The key is to know exactly which ones.

With regard to the focus of this book, I have found the following publications to be particularly informative and recommend you read them. Remember, you do not have to 'reinvent the wheel'.

Commodity Research Bureau (2004, 2005) *The CRB Commodity Yearbook*, John Wiley & Sons, New Jersey

Covel, Michael (2004) *Trend Following*, Prentice Hall, New Jersey

Edwards, Robert and Magee, John (1992) *Technical Analysis of Stock Trends*, New York Institute of Finance, New York

Koch, Richard (1997) *The 80/20 Principle*, Nicholas Brealey, London

Mackay, Charles (1932) *Extraordinary Popular Delusions and the Madness of Crowds*, Farrar, Straus & Giroux, New York

Murphy, John (1986) *Technical Analysis of the Futures Markets*, New York Institute of Finance, New York

Nofsinger, John (2001) *Investment Madness*, Prentice Hall, New Jersey

Schwager, Jack (1989) *Market Wizards*, New York Institute of Finance, New York

Schwager, Jack (1992) *The New Market Wizards*, New York Institute of Finance, New York

Sperandeo, Victor (1991) *Trader Vic*, John Wiley & Sons, New York

Sperandeo, Victor (1994) *Trader Vic II*, John Wiley & Sons, New York

Taleb, Nassim Nicholas (2001) *Fooled by Randomness*, Texere, New York

Index

Read Mark Shipman's investment diary every week on this free-access website

Mark Shipman is a master investor, who interposes common sense and strong research with a real command of his subject. After leaving the cushion of an employer's salary in 1990, he has amassed a personal fortune from backing his own judgement with his own money and has gained a reputation for identifying major investment trends during the early stages of their development.

There are not many people you can trust when it comes to investing because there are very few who have the knowledge and have actually made a success of it. That's why, when you find a successful investor revealing his thoughts and strategies, it pays to sit up and take notice.